WRITING A TEXTBOOK

How To Books on Successful Writing

Copyright & Law for Writers
Creating a Twist in the Tale
Creative Writing
How to be a Freelance Journalist
How to Publish a Book
How to Publish a Newsletter
How to Start Word Processing
How to Write a Press Release
How to Write & Sell Computer
  Software
How to Write for Publication
How to Write for Television
Improving Your Written English
Mastering Business English

Starting to Write
Writing & Publishing Poetry
Writing & Selling a Novel
Writing a Nonfiction Book
Writing a Report
Writing a Textbook
Writing an Assignment
Writing an Essay
Writing Business Letters
Writing Reviews
Writing Romantic Fiction
Writing Science Fiction, Fantasy
  & Horror
Writing Your Dissertation

Other titles in preparation

The How To series now contains more than 200 titles in the following categories:

Business Basics
Family Reference
Jobs & Careers
Living & Working Abroad
Student Handbooks
Successful Writing

Please send for a free copy of the latest catalogue for full details (see back cover for address).

SUCCESSFUL WRITING

WRITING
A TEXTBOOK

How to establish yourself as
an academic author

Penny Grubb and Danuta Reah

HAVE YOU FOUND A
WAY TO LINK THE
CHAPTERS?

How To Books

To Friends Mary (Aldbro') and
Ann (B'ham)

Cartoons by Mike Flanagan

British Library Cataloguing in Publication Data
A catalogue record for this book is available from the British Library.

First published in 1997 by How To Books Ltd, 3 Newtec Place,
Magdalen Road, Oxford OX4 1RE, United Kingdom.
Tel: (01865) 793806. Fax: (01865) 248780.

Note: The material contained in this book is set out in good faith for
general guidance and no liability can be accepted for loss or expense
incurred as a result of relying in particular circumstances on statements
made in the book. The laws and regulations are complex and liable to
change, and readers should check the current position with the relevant
authorities before making personal arrangements.

Produced for How To Books by Deer Park Productions.
Typeset by PDQ Typesetting, Stoke-on-Trent, Staffs.
Printed and bound by Cromwell Press, Broughton Gifford, Melksham,
Wiltshire.

Contents

List of Illustrations

Preface

Many potentially excellent textbooks are never written. Many people with knowledge and skills to share only ever pass on their wisdom to relatively small groups of people. Experienced teachers pass on their skills to class after class, year by year – but they could be reaching thousands. The ability and expertise of many of industry's most talented trainers is lost when people retire.

It is not a lack of knowledge or talent which stops people writing textbooks – these are the very things that make them potential authors of valuable books – it is the added baggage that goes with the writing of textbooks that stops many aspiring writers in their tracks: how and when to approach a publisher; how to frame the idea; how to research markets; how to translate from face-to-face teaching to the written word.

Writing a Textbook aims to take the pain out of the whole process; to lead the aspiring writer step-by-step through the stages from initial conception of the idea to a complete book proposal; and beyond that to the structuring and development of the book itself.

By following the book's ideas, suggestions and advice, the aspiring textbook writer is taken through the gradual building of the embryo textbook.

If you follow the book from start to finish and carry out the suggested tasks from chapter to chapter, you should end up with a fully fledged book proposal with which to approach a publisher.

If you succeed in winning a book contract you can then refer back to *Writing a Textbook* for advice on organising your writing schedule, setting and sticking to deadlines and adapting your style to suit the type of textbook you are creating.

Writing a Textbook is aimed at teachers and lecturers of any subject at any level: researchers, those with specialist expertise and experience, academic and commercial – anyone, in fact, with knowledge and skills to share.

Penny Grubb
Danuta Reah

1
Deciding the Academic Subject Area

This chapter gives guidance on:

- deciding which area of the academic market to target
- identifying areas within your target where a new textbook is needed
- focusing your book at existing courses or new areas
- creating a new angle to make your book attractive to your potential market.

TARGETING YOUR EXPERTISE

The function of a textbook is to pass on information and expertise on a particular topic from someone with a high level of knowledge or expertise to someone with a lower level of knowledge or expertise. As a potential textbook writer, you do not want to have to do extensive work developing a new area of expertise; you are, instead, targeting skills you already have in another or a wider direction.

> *Write about what you know.*

Recognising your market

Anyone who is an expert in a particular area has knowledge that people want. Writing a textbook is just another way of marketing your expertise. Your skill may be in a vocational area (building trades, catering, hairdressing, business) or it may be in an academic area (literature, philosophy, psychology, geology, astronomy). The one thing you can be certain of is that someone, somewhere, will want to learn that skill.

However, it is important to target your expertise carefully. For example:

- If you are aiming at the **schools market**, it is important to decide which age group you are targeting.

- If you are aiming at the **college market**, you need to know the specific requirements of that market.

- If you are aiming at the **higher education market**, you need to know how it differs from other markets.

- If you are aiming at the **international market** you need to familiarise yourself with the educational requirements of the countries you are targeting.

Targeting the schools market

Get to know this market and its requirements by familiarising yourself with the relevant qualifications system. If you are planning to write for English or Welsh schools, read the National Curriculum document and look at exam papers and test papers for the levels you are working in.

Remember that schools rarely have big enough budgets to buy books that are not directly relevant to the skills they have to teach.

If you are planning to write for Scottish schools, make yourself familiar with the requirements of the Scottish curriculum, or make sure that the book you write will be useful in Scottish, Welsh and English schools. See the Further Reading and Useful Addresses sections for details of where to obtain the curriculum documents.

Targeting the college market

If you are aiming at the college market, make sure you are familiar with the range of courses on offer.

Are you aware that as well as GCSE, A-Level and GNVQ, colleges offer access courses, Accreditation of Prior Learning, special needs courses, basic literacy and numeracy, core skills and also franchised higher education courses?

The college market differs from the school market, and it is important that your book is made directly relevant to this market. A lot of textbooks aimed at courses taught in both schools and colleges sell well to both markets, but you need to be aware of the requirements for both so you can balance your book on this fine line.

> *Don't produce a book that in the end appeals to neither market because your aim was too wide.*

Targeting higher education

If you are planning to write for the higher education market, you need to be aware of the core content of courses in your area. How many universities and colleges of higher education offer courses in your specialist area? Do you know what level of knowledge the students will need? Find out from a selection of university prospectuses or the *UCAS Handbook* (see the Useful Addresses section).

Remember that what can seem very basic to you as an expert can be very advanced even for a student at this level. Is your market likely to include foundation year students who will need a fairly basic introduction to the subject, or will they be more advanced?

The level of the students for whom you write is a key aspect and needs detailed consideration.

Targeting the international market

If you are aiming to sell internationally, aim to find where your largest market is likely to be.

Certain specialist areas are of more interest than others in certain parts of the world. For example, the Middle and Far East are good markets for English as a Foreign Language (EFL) books. Would your expertise best be targeted in this direction? English for Specific Purposes (ESP) is a very big market: English for engineers, English for computer scientists, English for international business – all of these areas and more are worth exploring.

Identify in particular:

- which specialist areas are in demand and where

- the requirements of the education system in the countries in which you are interested

- the levels at which your subject is taught

- the syllabuses that are taught.

See the Further Reading and Useful Addresses sections for pointers on where to find this information.

> *Find your market.*
> *Find out exactly what your market requires.*
> *Find out how your expertise can provide it.*

FINDING A GAP IN THE MARKET

Unless you are very lucky, a wide range of textbooks will already be available in your area. There is often no more room in the market for just another textbook, even if it is a very good one (like yours). The important thing to do is to identify a gap in the market, a place where a textbook is needed but hasn't yet been provided.

Your first step is get a general picture of the current competition. As you are working within your own area of expertise, you will be familiar with most of the important textbooks at your own level. However, you may decide to write your book for a different level, where you may not be so familiar with the books available. Use the information in the Further Reading and Useful Addresses sections to get a picture of what is, and what is not, currently available.

In addition, bookshops and libraries are useful places to look. A good academic bookshop will stock all the titles that are currently in demand. If you see a lot of books on your subject, don't despair. This means there is a big market.

Another useful place to look is *Books in Print* (see the Further Reading section), a bibliography of all current books in print, with a subject area classification. This will give you a snapshot of the current market.

However, publishers need to keep ahead of their market. It is very useful to get catalogues from publishers in your specialist area. These will give you an idea of what is forthcoming – soon to be available but not yet in print.

Using the Internet

If you plan to write for an international market, you will need to do wider market research. If you have access to the Internet, you should be able to find library catalogues for the areas you are interested in. See the Useful Addresses section for some relevant web pages.

- Identify publishers who publish for your chosen market, and send for their catalogues for the countries for which you plan to write.

- Write to education establishments in the countries you hope to target, asking them for student book lists for the courses in your area.

By these means, you will gain a useful idea of the potential size of your market and the likely competition.

Identifying the need for a new textbook
If you want a publisher to accept your book proposal, you need to be able to convince him or her that your book:

- is needed
- will sell
- is not just another competing title in an overcrowded field.

In other words, you need to identify a gap in the market. If you do your initial research thoroughly, you will be in a good position to do so.

There are many reasons why new textbooks are always needed:

- Most specialisms move on over time. This means that books become out of date.

- Teaching methods change, and textbook requirements change with them.

- Syllabuses change, and so a textbook that addresses an old syllabus will be less useful than one that addresses a new one.

- Some subjects are difficult to teach and difficult for students to grasp. You may have devised a teaching method that you know, from experience, really works.

- You may have devised a way of explaining a complex subject in a way that makes it interesting and accessible to the reader.

Changes in the specialist field
Reading the academic or professional journals relating to your field is important in keeping abreast of recent developments. If you are up to date, you will know how out of date current textbooks may be. Target your book proposal at the gap in expertise, so that your book will bring the subject up to date.

Changes in teaching methods

There have been major changes in the world of education over recent years. Economic constraints mean that schools, colleges and universities have to adopt a range of teaching methods that make the most efficient use of staff time.

Open and **distance learning** is a rapidly expanding and under-resourced market. Is there a demand in your area of expertise? **Resource based learning** is another developing area in which students expand the knowledge developed in class time via a range of self-study resources.

Current wrangles about the most effective teaching methods in schools mean that books that can be used flexibly by the teacher, for example in facilitating

- group work
- whole group teaching
- self-study
- rote learning,

will be more useful than books that assume one method.

There is also a tremendous demand in the school and college markets for photocopiable **resource packs** that effectively provide the teacher or lecturer with a series of timed and planned lessons that can be freely photocopied within the educational establishment.

Changes in syllabuses

Changes in syllabuses and the development of new syllabuses mean that there is always a demand for new textbooks. It is important to be aware of changes before they happen, as publishers need to get the appropriate books on the market in time for the start of a new syllabus. It is important to know what teaching time-scales schools, colleges and universities are using.

For example, schools teach most GCSE and A-Level subjects over two years. Your book needs to be on the market two years before the first new exam. Colleges, on the other hand, usually take only one year to teach a GCSE, and either one or two years to teach an A-Level, so if you are targeting the mature student at this level, your book needs to be on the market at least one year before the first exam. Publishers will be commissioning new books with this time-scale in mind.

Traditionally 'difficult' subjects

If your expertise is in an area that has a reputation for being difficult, dry and with a low success rate – the hard sciences, for example – some of the problems may lie with the current textbooks or the current teaching methods. In this case, your textbook can capture a market share by being different. For example, it may:

- help teenagers to see how fascinating maths and physics really are

- offer a teacher a new and effective approach to interest a class

- offer a university lecturer useful material for helping students into a demanding subject area

- help fill in the gaps that exist between courses taught at pre-university level and first year degree courses.

> *All of these are points to bear in mind when you are looking at your potential market and trying to identify your slot.*

DECIDING UPON THE SCOPE

Once you have identified the gap in the market that your book will fill, it will be easier to decide on the scope that your book will cover. This will also depend, of course, on your target audience and level.

Sometimes your expertise can get in the way of clear decision making here. You know how large your subject area is, and the depth of knowledge required to get a real grip on it. You need to think about this carefully from the point of view of the audience for whom you are writing. What stage are they starting from and where should they be at the end?

Avoiding the pitfalls

There are two potential pitfalls here for you as the writer:

1. Deciding to cover the whole of your area. You don't feel able to select the knowledge and level your audience requires. The end result will be one of two things: a book so long no publisher will look at it because it would be prohibitively expensive; or a book that may give a comprehensive outline of the area, but goes into so little depth it is of limited use to its audience.

2.   Focusing on a narrow area. This is the one that experts who are not teachers are likely to fall into. You will have your own particular areas of interest within your subject area, and your inclination is to focus on that area to the exclusion of others. For a textbook, this is rarely a useful approach. This is one of the major differences between writing a textbook and writing academic papers (see Chapter 10). Your book will give a very in-depth coverage of your specific area of interest, but the book as a whole is likely to be far too narrow to interest a publisher.

Putting yourself in the position of your audience and deciding what they need is an essential exercise. It will help you to decide how best to break the subject down into a series of levels and targets for each level.

Start at the level of expertise your readers will have (or slightly below to give some support to readers slightly below the expected level) and take your book to the level you want your readers to be at when they have finished the book.

The publisher may not require a specific aims and objectives list to appear in your book (though many do), but such a list will be invaluable to you in deciding the scope of your book. If you can't produce one for your own use, you haven't yet focused your ideas sufficiently closely.

It is also worth profiling your target audience according to level, skills and knowledge.

Profiling your target audience

Level
Are they beginners, do they have some previous background, have they studied the area for some time, are they experts in their own right? Being absolutely clear in your own mind about this will keep your textbook at the right level.

Previous knowledge
Do they know specific background topics? If so, your book can build on this knowledge. If not, you may have to develop certain background areas.

On what are you basing your assumptions about previous knowledge? Are you certain that it is reasonable for you to assume your audience has this?

Previous skills

Do they have specific background skills? If so, you can assume that your readership can use these skills.

Analyse why you assume they will have these skills. Remember that the skills you are expecting your audience to have need not only be those relating to the subject area. They may be expected to have wider skills such as close reading skills, research skills, presentation skills or IT skills. These are usually referred to as **core skills**. It is important that you are aware of the level of core skills your readership is likely to have.

Audience profile for a book on text analysis for A-Level and first year undergraduates:

Level: A-Level and first year HE.

Previous knowledge: some knowledge of language structure – word classes, phrase, clause and sentence structure; awareness of language varieties.

Previous skills: reading attentively with comprehension; adapting text for different audiences and functions; applying knowledge of language structure to a variety of texts.

Fig. 1. Audience profile for a textbook.

You can use this information as shown in Figure 1 to help you to decide on an appropriate scope for your book that will make it invaluable to potential students, and attractive to your market.

WRITING A SPECIFIC COURSE BOOK

It is often easier to answer the above questions if you are writing a book for a specific course.

Many textbooks arise from a teacher's own experience, and often the most popular textbooks for specific courses are those written by practising teachers using material and ideas that have been developed and trialled in the classroom or lecture theatre.

If you are planning to follow this route – that is, use your own teaching material as a basis for a textbook – you still need to go through the processes outlined above to identify a gap in the market.

You may find that you need to develop a new angle to make your proposal fill an existing gap.

If you are planning to target your book at a specific course, but you are not a teacher or involved in the teaching profession, your first question is likely to be *which course*? Are you familiar with the range of courses taught in your subject area? Are you familiar with likely changes that may occur to courses in the foreseeable future?

If you are thinking of writing for the schools market for the pre-16 age group, for example, make sure that your area is a National Curriculum area at the level for which you plan to write. There is very little point in deciding that children need a particular area of expertise if it is not taught in the schools. (You may well be right, but you won't sell your book to the education market.)

Whatever level you plan to write for, make sure you are aware of all the courses that are taught within your area at that level. Remember that there are not only the well-known national courses such as SATs, GCSE, A-Level, GNVQ, NVQ, BA and BSc, but there are also a wide range of other courses that may require textbooks specifically aimed at them.

For a list of places to contact to find out about courses, see the Useful Addresses section.

This research should give you a reasonably comprehensive list of courses in your specialism, including courses aimed at school children, students, special needs, teachers, trainers and professionals.

Getting started

When you have decided which course you want to tackle, you need to:

- get a copy of the syllabus

- read publications aimed at professionals in the area

- find out what developments are expected in the field

- talk to people who are teaching the course

- find out what specific requirements these teachers have

- talk to students and find out their needs.

This will equip you with the information that will enable you to convert your expertise into a textbook for a specific course.

TACKLING A NEW FIELD

New developments in education or new market requirements may mean that your specialism moves into a wider area than it has previously occupied. This means that the textbook market in your area expands dramatically.

A good example of this is the developments in Information Technology (IT) that made it a core skill at all levels of the education system. An IT expert with an eye on the market was therefore ideally placed to benefit from this change.

Another example is that of theoretical linguistics, a small and rather esoteric area of higher education that has expanded in popularity in the last 15 years under a range of influences, including the development of a popular A-Level in English Language that included some knowledge of theoretical linguistics. There has been a massive expansion of textbooks in this area in recent years.

Try to be aware of any potential developments that may affect your area in this way. The first textbook on the market in any new area will usually soak up the market for a while, as desperate teachers and trainers look for books that will help them to develop and teach a new course.

CREATING A NEW ANGLE

Sometimes, despite all the research you do, you may not be able to identify a gap in the market. Your area seems to be well supplied with textbooks at all the levels you can identify. Is this the point to give up?

Why did you decide in the first place to write a textbook? Was it because you, or people you knew who were involved in teaching the subject, thought that there was a need? Was it because you felt you had specialist knowledge to pass on to others? Most people who decide to write a textbook do so because they have a gut feeling that the existing market is not sufficient, and that gut feeling is usually correct.

Creating your own gap in the market

Deciding what your textbook will have that other textbooks lack is a way of identifying the less obvious gaps in the market. For example, the current textbooks may not engage the interest of the student or may not deliver the information in the most accessible way. If you have a new angle, this may be enough to convince the publisher that your book is needed.

Why some textbooks fail

The psychology of learning is a large and complex subject. One important factor in successful teaching and learning is the motivation of the learner. If the learner is a conscript rather than a volunteer, then motivation may well be non-existent, and successful learning will not take place. This is largely a problem for the teacher, but the textbook writer can address this problem. If he or she does this successfully then the book will be a success.

An example from core skills gives a useful illustration. Many students have to develop skills in areas that they would not, by themselves, choose to follow. Students in countries where English is not the first language will often be expected to learn English along with their chosen subject.

One such course involved teaching English to students who were training to be engineers. They were aware of the need for English, but they gave it a low priority and the success rate was low.

An imaginative collaboration between the experts in the two fields – English for Specific Purposes and Engineering – solved the problem. The students, instead of being taught English, were given the project of designing and building a box-kite. They had to write a manual for both the design and use of the kite – in English.

Their skills in both areas developed.

Be imaginative!

If you think that a new and radical approach is needed for teaching your specialism at the level you have chosen, do not be afraid to develop it via your textbook.

When you approach a publisher with your proposal, make sure you can demonstrate the weaknesses that you see in existing textbooks, and the way in which your textbook addresses the problem.

CHECKLIST

- List your major areas of expertise. In which of these areas might there be a textbook?

- Make a list of courses available in your subject area at the level for which you want to produce a book. What sorts of numbers take these courses each year, and how widely are they available – locally, nationally or internationally?

QUESTION AND ANSWER

I have found a gap in the market in my area of expertise, where I think there really should be a textbook. Unfortunately, it overlaps into another area where I don't feel so confident. What should I do?

There are two possible solutions here. One is to collaborate with an expert from this other area. A lot of very successful textbooks are the result of joint authorship. A second solution is to research this area yourself and include it. You shouldn't then make this aspect the main focus of the book. A lot of textbook writing will involve research into related areas.

CASE STUDIES

Amanda decides to develop her teaching notes

Amanda has been teaching a specific course for several years. 'I've really got this cracked,' she tells a colleague. 'I'm going to write a book.'

She puts her full course teaching notes together and writes an outline to be sent to a publisher. She gives it to one of her colleagues. 'Would you just have a quick look at this for me and tell me what you think?'

Later in the week, she sees her colleague. 'Well,' she asks cheerfully, 'what do you think?'

'It's very good,' her colleague replies, 'and if we had it in the college library now, I'd use it. But I wouldn't buy it, and to be honest, I wouldn't advise the college to buy it.'

Amanda is hurt. 'Why not?' she says.

'You can't have forgotten,' her colleague replies. 'The whole syllabus changes in two years. This book will be out of date as soon as that happens. It would be a waste of money to buy it.'

Amanda has forgotten that extensive syllabus changes are due and her proposal doesn't address them.

Barry spots a gap in the international market

Barry has recently been doing a lot of reading in the course of his work. There have been a lot of exciting new developments in his field, and his own research has given him a lot of expertise in this area. He mentions this to a colleague.

'It's all very well for you to get excited,' his colleague grumbles, 'but it means that we're going to have to spend a fortune on books to bring our students up to date.'

'Don't they cover this before they come to us?' Barry asks.

'I don't think so,' says his colleague.

Barry knows that a lot of the students who do courses in his department are from other countries. He looks at some of the course books that are recommended. None of them is as up-to-date as Barry's research. He contacts colleagues working in the same area at different universities. They all have a large intake of overseas students.

Barry discusses with his colleague a proposal for a textbook that will cover this new area.

'I think there is a big market here for this book,' he says. 'Our own home market needs it, some of our undergraduates need a good introduction because they aren't getting it before they come to us, and there is a big market overseas, if our own student intake is anything to go by.'

'Couldn't existing books be updated?'

'They'll need extensive rewriting,' Barry tells him. 'I think that this field is ripe for a completely new book.'

Barry uses his contacts to spot a gap in the international market.

Clare uses her specialist knowledge

Ever since Clare retired, her ex-colleagues have been 'borrowing' her expertise. 'Why do you keep on coming to me?' she asks one in exasperation.

'It's the problems we have training graduates up,' he says. 'We're happy with their theoretical knowledge, but they're very weak on the practical side. You're the only person who really knows how to train them.'

'Isn't there a textbook you could use with them?' Clare asks.

'No,' is the reply.

Clare decides that if her expertise is going to be used, she will be the one who profits. She decides to write a textbook, and gets out all her old training notes and materials that she developed while she was working for her last company. 'Some of this is out-of-date,' she thinks, 'but there is still a lot I can use.'

She writes a proposal and shows it to a friend who works in the same field. She is surprised when her friend is not enthusiastic. 'I don't know why,' she complains to the next ex-colleague who comes seeking her advice.

'I don't know a lot about it,' he says, 'but I wonder if it's because each company has different problems in this area – and you've written an outline for a book for one company, not for all of them.'

'I think you may be right,' says Clare. 'I need to think about this a bit more.'

Clare's proposal is just too narrow at this stage.

DISCUSSION POINTS

1. What are the aims and objectives of the book you intend to write?

2. Who is your target audience?

3. What kind of person would read your book?

2
Approaching an Academic Publisher

This chapter gives guidance on:

- identifying the academic publishers who will be interested in your textbook

- when and how to approach academic publishers

- assembling the material that will convince a publisher of the viability of your textbook.

FINDING A PUBLISHER – WHO TO APPROACH

As with submitting any material for publication, you must identify an appropriate publisher or agent. For example, it is no use sending your textbook proposal to a publisher who deals solely with children's fiction. This sounds obvious but any publisher will tell you that many people still submit material that is wholly inappropriate.

Apart from anything else, submitting to an inappropriate publisher is an admission that you haven't done your homework– hardly an auspicious start for one aiming to write textbooks.

Many who aspire to textbook writing will already have a good working knowledge of appropriate publishers through the books they read as part of their work.

Make use of the knowledge you already have.

Identifying your priorities

Different publishers have different things to offer. In order to get the best deal, you need to know what you want.

Are fame and fortune your top priority? Textbooks can be money spinners if they have wide enough appeal. Royalty deals vary enormously and it is up to you to judge where your interests lie.

A publisher like the Open University Press will usually offer a smaller royalty than a specialist scientific publisher, for example, but will be tapping a bigger market and make more sales. Generally, you would be looking in the range of 5 per cent to 15 per cent.

Do not dismiss the very small publishing houses. Some are prepared to take on texts for niche markets and have been known to offer up to 50 per cent royalties.

Asking the right questions

When you discuss the idea for your book with a publisher's representative, he or she will have plenty of questions for you. After you have worked your way through *Writing a Textbook*, you should have the answers at your fingertips.

However, you should also have questions for the publisher. Long before you have a contract put in front of you for signature, you want to know if this will be the right deal.

Ask – earlier rather than later.

What are your priorities? What is important to you? What do you need to know about a publisher? Think these things through and go into your meetings armed with a list of questions. An example is given in Figure 2, but you are the only one who knows what is really important to you, so you must create your own list.

Find out from the rep:

What is the usual royalty deal?

What sales do you expect to make?

How will you publicise the book?

What is your track record for this type of book in the international market?

What was your best selling book last year?

Fig. 2. Some questions for the publisher.

Identifying your options

You know what your priorities are. You have a good idea what type of deal you want. What you need to do now is to maximise your chances of getting that deal. To do this, you need to identify all your options. Done fully, this is a time-consuming task but it can pay dividends. Later in this chapter, shortcuts for those who *really* don't have the time are discussed.

First you need to compile a list of all the publishers who might be interested in publishing your textbook. The Useful Addresses and Further Reading sections in this book will give you a starting point.

Check this list against the priorities that you have identified and eliminate those publishers who fall short of the criteria you have set. For example:

- If you are aiming specifically at the international market, some of the smaller publishing houses will be inappropriate.

- If your proposed book has a wide general appeal, look for a publisher who can tap a wide market.

- If you are writing in a specialist field, look for the publishers already in that field – they will have the right contacts to publicise and sell your book.

- If your book is to be targeted towards a specific level – first year undergraduate, for example – look for the publishers who have experience in this specific market.

- If the content and level of your proposed book gives it a narrow, clearly defined potential audience – for example, National Curriculum Key Stage 1 has a large but precisely defined audience and is not suitable for the international market – consider in particular the smaller publishing houses. The Useful Addresses section gives some tips on how to find them.

---

*Identifying **all** your options gives you the greatest chance of identifying your **best** option.*

When time is of the essence

The identification of a publisher is actually quite a sticking point.

Some embryo textbooks have perished right here when their authors simply haven't found the time for the initial research. Yes, it *is* better to do the job thoroughly and the work you do will stand you in good stead for all your subsequent books, but you can shortcut the process if absolutely necessary.

If you can identify a single publisher who is interested, then you can get your book off the ground. It might not be the best deal, it might not be the ideal publisher to target your intended audience but one interested publisher is better than no publisher at all.

You know your subject. If you didn't, you wouldn't be contemplating a textbook. You therefore have a good working knowledge of the relevant textbooks already published. Go and get one of them: the best written, the best seller, your own favourite, the one nearest to your own topic or just the one that happens to be nearest to hand. The publisher of this book is the first on your list.

You cannot guarantee to identify the best possible option by taking short cuts, but at least you have made a start.

TIMING IT RIGHT – WHEN TO APPROACH

If you have never approached a publisher before, it can be hard to decide exactly when to make the first move. If you approach too early, with insufficient information, there will be nothing on which the publisher can base a decision. Further, you will have wasted both his time and yours. Nonetheless, an early approach can be valuable.

You should not approach a publisher before you have a clear initial idea for a textbook, but you should approach as soon as possible afterwards.

You should approach:

- **With the initial idea** when the idea is clear in your own mind. This initial approach will let you know whether or not to continue with this particular publisher. Do not expect a firm decision at this stage, but you should get a good indication. As well as the idea, you should have had thoughts on the potential market for your text.

- **With the full proposal** after the initial meeting and after having been given the green light to take the idea forward. The publisher will provide a proposal pro-forma. Although these pro-formas vary in structure, the information required is very much the same.

If you follow the guidance notes and checklists as you go through *Writing a Textbook*, you should finish the book with all the material you need to construct a textbook for any publisher.

- **With sample material** when asked. You may be asked to submit sample material at various different points: before an initial decision is taken, with the book proposal or after the proposal has been accepted. The one thing you can guarantee is that you will be asked at some stage. Specific sections in *Writing a Textbook* are aimed at leading you through the construction of individual chapters.

ASSEMBLING THE RIGHT MATERIAL – HOW TO APPROACH

The textbook proposal, and how to construct its various elements is covered in detail throughout *Writing a Textbook*. In general the rule to follow is:

> *Provide the material that is requested, in the format that is requested and when it is requested.*

If you are asked for an **outline** of the whole book, do not provide a sample chapter. If you are given a sample layout and style, follow it exactly. Authors who do not follow house rules make extra work for the publisher. Failing to follow instructions on the format of a book proposal will not automatically mean that your idea will be rejected, but it certainly won't help to dispose a publisher in your favour.

Are you convinced that you have a good and viable idea for a textbook? If so, then aim to convince the publisher at every step along the way. Stress the **positive** – the potential in an expanding market, the international aspect, the gap in the market that you have identified. *You* know why your textbook can be a success. It is up to you to get the message across to the potential publisher.

If you are not convinced by your own idea, then go back to the drawing board. If you can't convince yourself, you won't convince a publisher.

> *To get your textbook off the ground, you have to interest a publisher. Aim to get the following three areas right:*
> ***who, when** and **how**.*

CHECKLIST

- Make a list of publishers relevant to the subject area of your proposed textbook. Look specifically for the publishers of books that you find useful in this field, but investigate more widely by using such tools as Year Books or comprehensive lists of books in print – see the Further Reading section for further details.

- List up to six books on the same subject or in the same subject area as your proposed textbook. For each, write a paragraph saying how the book would or would not suit the people identified in the Discussion Points of Chapter 1.

QUESTION AND ANSWER

I approached a publisher's representative some time ago. She was very interested and said she would send me a proposal form. I've heard nothing since. What should I do?

Follow it up. The representative you spoke to may have since left the company, or may have been busy and forgotten you. Ring the publishers and tell them that their representative was interested in your ideas.

CASE STUDIES

Amanda tries a random stab in the dark
'I don't believe this,' storms Amanda, brandishing a newly opened letter. 'They've turned me down without even asking for further details.'

'Which publisher did you approach?' asks a colleague.

Amanda hands him the letter. He looks at it and asks, 'What made you go to these people?'

'Well, they published that series we used to use at level three. I thought they'd be interested in good practical texts.'

'But that was years ago. Haven't they been taken over? I thought they mostly did fiction these days.'

Amanda returns to her desk looking thoughtful. It has occurred to her that the memorable series of books she was thinking of were actually very different in content and level from her own text. Her anger at the publishers evaporates and she feels annoyed with herself instead for giving so little thought to her choice of publisher.

Barry doesn't know what to prepare – but goes ahead anyway

Barry marches confidently into his first meeting with the publisher's representative. He has already established that the publisher is willing to consider his idea seriously and has spent the previous week preparing material for this meeting.

'Give me an outline of the subject area,' says the rep.

Barry hands across a sheaf of papers. 'This will give you an overall picture of...' The rep interrupts, waving the papers aside, 'Just tell me in your own words, briefly.'

Barry complies, referring to his notes as he expands upon his topic. Again, the rep's upraised hand stops him. 'I don't want this level of detail. I know nothing about the subject. Just give me an outline.'

Feeling a little put out, Barry does his best. He then tries to interest the rep in the material he has prepared – the sample chapter, the detailed outline, the résumé of the background research area – but the rep says, 'Where will your book sell? Who is going to want to buy it?'

Barry flounders. Though confident of the book's saleability, he hasn't give much thought to this aspect.

At the end of the meeting, the rep tells Barry that it is worth his while to submit a proposal and he hands Barry a proposal form.

Barry is pleased that things have been taken a stage further but he is rather dismayed by the contents of the form. Much of the material he has prepared is of no use at all, some he will be able to use but will have to restructure and he had not even thought of many of the areas.

Instead of being over the moon at having been asked to submit a proposal, he is depressed at the thought of the time he has wasted.

Clare does her research

'Which publisher will you go to?'

'I haven't decided yet,' says Clare, holding up a long list, 'but it will be one of these.'

'Where on earth did you get all those from?' asks her friend, amazed.

'These are all the publishers who might take work in the area. These are the international ones, these the national, and these the local. Then I've also classified them according to their major market – academic, commercial and so on. The figures are recent sales of comparable books where I've been able to find the information.'

'Is all that really necessary?'

'Oh yes, it'll be worth it in the end. I expect to shortlist a dozen or so and I'd expect at least half of those to be prepared to offer me a contract.'

'Can't be bad,' laughs her friend, 'fighting for the privilege of publishing you.'

'It's a lot of tedious work, I know,' says Clare, 'but I'll reap the benefit in the long term by getting the deal I want.'

DISCUSSION POINTS

1. Who publishes the books that you use most in your area of work?

2. Are there any particular publishers who produce a lot of the material you need?

3. Are there any small publishers in your locality – independent or attached to local universities or colleges?

3
Drawing Up a Realistic Schedule

This chapter gives guidance on:

- strategies for timetabling the writing of a textbook
- planning
- setting milestones
- fixing realistic deadlines
- some of the common pitfalls.

WRITING THE TIMETABLE

Potential publishers will ask you how long it will take to finish your textbook and it is best to have a realistic answer ready. If you guess, you will almost certainly underestimate the time needed.

Even when your book is little more than a nebulous idea, you can make some estimates about its final length and structure.

As a first effort towards a timetable, you will need to:

- list the major topics you wish to cover

- estimate for each of these the depth in which you will cover it

- assess the need for extra research for each topic – do you have all the information at your fingertips? Do you need access to information and material not immediately at hand?

Estimating the number of chapters

From the above, you can make a first attempt to enumerate the chapters – topics covered in brief may be estimated as single chapters or possibly part chapters, topics covered in depth should be estimated as one chapter per major sub-topic.

This will give you a rough estimate of the number of chapters in the body of your textbook. Add another three: one for the introduction, one for the conclusion and one 'for luck'. This final 'lucky' chapter will cover such areas as the preface, the acknowledgements, the references and may also have to stretch to cover an extra chapter that hadn't occurred to you at this early stage.

Estimating a completion date

If you have to give a proposed date for completion based only on a roughly estimated timetable – and sometimes this will happen – a rough guide is to estimate between four and six weeks per chapter and double the final figure. Hence, if you estimate eleven chapters and estimate a month for each, your estimated completion date should be almost two years away.

As you work towards a full proposal and contract, you will be able to refine the timetable and this estimated delivery date is likely to come nearer, which is better than a completion date which gets further and further away.

If you estimate completion in two years but actually deliver in 18 months, you will please both yourself and your publisher far more than promising delivery in a year and being six months behind schedule.

SETTING MILESTONES

A realistic and workable schedule will take much of the strain out of the writing process. Creating such a schedule means identifying the important milestones.

Start and end dates

The submission date gives you your target. Milestones on the route towards this are:

- the book structure – deciding the overall contents and outline

- the chapters – one milestone per chapter

- the completed first draft.

Aim to complete the first draft at least a couple of weeks (preferably a month) before the submission date.

A date for finalising the book structure – your start date – depends very much how far along the way you are already. You may already have passed this milestone before writing your timetable. If so, your start date is now.

Taking the end date as the submission date, set each chapter milestone at regular intervals between the start and end dates. It is always prudent to allow an extra chapter at the end when doing this. Set an actual date for each milestone.

Making initial adjustments
Some chapters will take longer than the time allowed, for instance if an element of research is going to be needed. Other chapters will take less where, for instance, the topic is based on notes you have already written. You should amend your timetable, within the fixed points of the start and end dates, to reflect this.

Draft milestones

Now, for each chapter milestone, set another – a draft milestone. The original date is the date that the chapter should be all but complete. The draft milestone would usually be at least a week beforehand. This milestone is the date by which you should have all the information written up, but not necessarily structured in exactly the way it should be.

STICKING TO THE TIMETABLE

Using your diary

Write all the milestones into your diary. This way, you can see where the book will fit in with the rest of your commitments. As well as noting the milestone dates, schedule time to complete each task. If you plan to spend three half days per week on your book during a particular period, then write those half days into your diary (see Figure 3).

Treat these diary entries just like meetings and appointments. Suppose someone rings and asks, 'Can you meet me tomorrow afternoon at two to discuss...?' You would have no hesitation in replying 'No, I have a board meeting then.' However, if a glance at your diary shows 'work on chapter 1 of textbook', the temptation is to say 'Yes, I can spare ten minutes.'

Fight that temptation. For the hours set aside to work on your book, your door should be closed, your colleagues should be aware that you are busy and not to be disturbed. If you can, divert your phone calls – writing needs concentration, you can't do it by snatching an odd five minutes here and there.

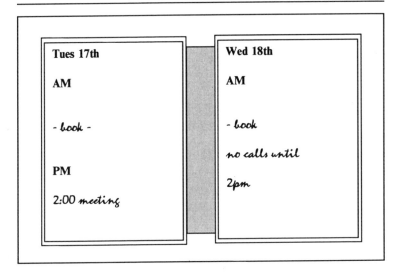

Fig. 3. Using the diary.

The draft and major chapter milestones

The time between the draft and major milestone for each chapter is for:

- re-structuring
- editing
- giving a final polish.

If anything more crops up – an extra topic needs to be added, more research needs to be done, new sections are needed – make a note, but do not tackle these things at the expense of missing the major milestone. Polish what is there. The big repairs are best tackled at the end – during the time allowed for that extra chapter, or sooner if another milestone is reached early.

AGREEING A DEADLINE FOR DELIVERY

You should always draw up a timetable before agreeing a deadline for delivery. Even a timetable based on guesswork is better than no timetable. Go through the whole process of setting milestones and assigning dates to them. By doing this you can go through your diary and check that you haven't missed anything major.

You do not want to be approaching a milestone for a major chapter when you are away on holiday. A deadline for delivery should not coincide with a major deadline at work. You should aim to be doing the bulk of the work on your book when you have as few other commitments as possible.

The time taken to write a textbook varies from months to years. The average textbook, in so far as there is such a thing, takes between a year and 18 months.

You do not know what might happen between now and the completion date for your book. Many things can serve as major disrupters of the most carefully thought out timetable. You may change your job, someone else's bad planning may land you with a major task at an inappropriate time. The only way to handle this is to allow extra leeway for the unexpected. Do this via such means as allowing for an extra chapter and putting work time as well as deadline dates into your diary.

AVOIDING THE COMMON PITFALLS

Good planning can mean the difference between writing a whole book to schedule and never getting beyond chapter two. Some pitfalls in the way of a good plan are:

- forgetting the diary

- not incorporating house rules

- giving no thought to structure

- duplicating effort if there is more than one author

- falling victim to stress.

Forgetting the diary

If you decide that you can write a chapter in a week starting from 1 March, do not automatically assume that the chapter will be finished by the 7th.

What do you mean by a week? Five eight-hour days? Seven eight-hour days? What if you have an important meeting on 3 March for which you have to travel to a different city – that's a day to prepare, a day spent at the meeting, a day to write up your report. That is three days out of your week.

What about that staff meeting on the Friday afternoon and those two lectures to prepare and deliver?

Between 1 and 7 March, you may have no more than four hours to spare for your book – half a day.

A week to write the chapter may well be realistic, but unless you are taking a holiday for the express purpose of writing, do not assume that seven days equals a week's worth of writing time.

Leaving house rules for later

A publisher will give you various instructions regarding the style and structuring of your book. These may include:

- guidance on chapter lengths

- a specific style for footnotes and references

- formats for illustrations and diagrams.

Take careful note of all these things when you start. It is far easier to build the house style in from the start than to have to cope with altering the completed manuscript.

Giving no thought to structure

You should give thought to book structure and your own house style as soon as possible. A mass of unstructured notes for a particular chapter does not constitute a draft.

A comprehensive mass of notes may signify that your research for this chapter is done. The *next* step is to structure and develop these notes into the draft chapter.

Textbook chapters flow one from another. You must give thought to structure as you work through the book, otherwise your chapters will not hang together. Chapters left as unstructured notes to a late stage invariably lead to further restructuring of related chapters.

Having to re-do chapters that you had thought were finished plays havoc with the timetable.

Duplicating effort

Chapters in a textbook will usually deal with closely related material. Decisions need to be made about exactly where specific topics will be covered in depth, otherwise there is a danger of duplicating work. This is a particular danger where there is more than one author.

Multi-authored texts usually benefit from extra work in the planning stage. Chapters should be planned in more detail prior to being drafted to prevent duplication. In a complex text, this is a useful exercise to see that topics are covered in an appropriate order. This will not extend the total time needed, rather it will relocate the planning stage for each of the chapters.

Falling victim to stress

Many who have the potential to write textbooks are already in high stress jobs. The last thing they need is to add to those stress levels. Remember, a good schedule is invaluable. It allows you to pace yourself.

Are you falling behind schedule...?
A good schedule shows you if you are falling behind. The advantage is that you get to know immediately and have a structure within which to catch up. You can retrieve the situation with the minimum of worry.

...or not?
Thinking that you are falling behind is a cause of stress. A good schedule gives concrete assurance that you are bang up to date!

CHECKLIST

- Draw up a timetable based on your current free time.

- Identify possible reviewers for your proposed textbook:
    - those who would agree to act as informal reviewers *eg* friends and colleagues
    - those whom a publisher could call upon to carry out a formal review *eg* professionals in the field.

QUESTION AND ANSWER

There has been a major reshuffle at work and I have had to take on extra responsibilities. I'm not sure that I can keep to the delivery timetable for my book. If I tell the publisher, will they terminate my contract?

They are genuinely interested in your book or they would not have given you a contract in the first place. Therefore, they are unlikely to terminate it. First, reschedule your time. Any unexpected upheaval in home or working life can leave planned schedules in tatters. Re-do your timetable around your new responsibilities and when you have new deadlines worked out, contact your publishers and explain the situation.

CASE STUDIES

Amanda uses her teaching experience to good effect

Amanda spends most of her free afternoon poring over her diary and over the school timetables whilst making copious notes. A colleague asks what she is doing:

'I'm working out a timetable for writing this textbook,' she explains.

'Seems a lot of trouble to go to. How long will it take?'

'I need three months to get it written.'

'Then you've got your completion date wrong,' her colleague points to her notes. 'You've given yourself nearly 18 months.'

'I meant three months' solid writing. I've got to plan round my classes, my admin work, my course preparation and so on.'

'Even so, surely 18 months is excessive, not to mention a whole afternoon just planning a schedule?'

'Yes, I would have thought about a year if I'd had to guess. I'm really glad I checked up in detail. And I definitely haven't wasted this afternoon. In fact, I'd like to bet that I've saved myself several weeks and considerable worry.'

Her colleague leaves looking unconvinced but Amanda just smiles and murmurs, 'Wait till you've been in this job as long as I have.'

Barry is over-ambitious

'I think you have a deadline clash here, Barry,' his supervisor says, looking at Barry's two schedules.

Barry looks at his schedules. 'That's not a clash,' he says. 'The research deadline is a week before the chapter deadline.'

'Yes, but you haven't left yourself any time for final proofing.'

'That's what I've left the week's gap for.'

'But you have tutorial work the following week. When are you going to do that?'

'I hadn't put tutorial preparation in, it didn't seem relevant.'

'Relevant or not, it has to be done. Just because your research and your book are your two main priorities, it doesn't mean you can ignore other things. If you do, you'll find your schedule in tatters.'

Barry becomes rather thoughtful. He has just spotted another rather tight deadline cutting right across a week's holiday he has booked in the summer.

He needs no further encouragement to re-think his plans.

Clare makes a full-time job out of it

Clare discusses her proposed work schedule with a friend.

'It's very ambitious,' the friend says doubtfully.

Clare sighs. 'That's what everyone's telling me. But the thing is that I want to get on with it. I want to do it full-time. I used to work full-time, why on earth can't I write full-time?'

'I bet you never had quite such a punishing schedule as that when you were at work. You barely seem to have room for coffee breaks.'

Clare is already reconsidering. In her initial enthusiasm she concedes she may have overdone it.

'By all means work to this schedule if you want to,' advises her friend, 'but for heaven's sake, don't commit yourself to any external deadlines on the strength of it. One of your major aims is to enjoy writing this book. Don't let it become a millstone.'

DISCUSSION POINTS

1. Identify the times of day when you feel most creative.

2. List the major tasks you have to complete over the next six months.

3. What are your priorities over the next six months? Include the tasks you have just listed.

4
Designing the Framework

This chapter gives guidance on:

- keeping your textbook a cohesive whole, not a fragmentary mess

- leading the reader through the text so they get the most from it

- the importance of formulating clear and concise aims and objectives.

KEEPING THE AIM IN SIGHT

Textbooks have aims at different levels. The book as a whole has a specific aim, to impart a particular body of knowledge perhaps, or to promote understanding, or to provoke thought and discussion. Working towards the overall aim, each chapter has its own goal. Within this, each section of each chapter should have a purpose.

Identify your book's major aims, determine how each chapter works towards these aims and, within the chapters, decide how the chapter will flow towards its specific goal.

You, as the writer, must keep the aims clearly in front of you. If you fail to do this, you will not be able to make clear to the reader where the book is going. The reader must also be able to work through the book without ever having to stop and wonder, why am I reading about this subject, why have we jumped to this area?

If readers' minds can be focused so that they can concentrate fully on the specific purpose of the section they are reading, they will get maximum benefit from the book, with minimum effort. And that is one of the qualities which will make a textbook sell.

LEADING THE READER THROUGH THE TEXT

A vital part of good textbook writing is the ability to lead the reader through the text.

Why is it necessary to lead the reader? It is because a textbook has a specific purpose. It has information to impart, it should leave the reader with a deeper understanding, or a greater knowledge – a good novel can make do with leaving behind it the feeling of satisfaction that comes from a good read. A textbook must do more. It should leave knowledge, ideas and understanding in its readers' minds. Further, it should allow the reader back to sample selectively.

Every moment the readers spend wondering why this topic has followed from that, or where this or that section is leading, is time taken from their absorbing the substance of the book.

> *Never leave the textbook reader in suspense.*

Linking

Linking allows readers to find the material they want, when they want it. You cannot explain every significant topic that you mention, every time you mention it. However, you need to cater for the reader who wants or needs an explanation. Give the reader a link. Tell him or her where to find the information. If you cover the topic at some point in the book, say so. If not, tell the reader where to go to find it, for example:

- as detailed in the following chapter
- as was explained fully in Chapter 1
- see section 5.4
- see Reah and Ross (Reah 96) Chapter 10, for a full description.

And here is a genuine link – the subject of linking is covered in further detail in the next chapter.

Signposting

The reader of a textbook needs to be able to dip in anywhere and know where he or she is. A textbook may be read through from start to finish the first time round, but after that it is more likely to be used as a reference. Books which are easy to use as reference texts are especially useful – to the student studying for an exam, to the researcher wanting to home in on a specific topic – and hence more in demand.

To allow the book to be opened at any place with the readers knowing at once where they are, there must be signposts. There are different ways of signposting a textbook:

- **Sections and sub-sections** – wherever the book is opened, there will be a section or sub-section header to show the reader where in the text he is. As a reader becomes more and more familar with a text, the more familiar and thus more useful these signposts become.

- **Margin notes** – key words or phrases can be put into the margins to indicate the significance of each section. This is a useful means of signposting long blocks of text.

Cohesion

Nothing will disorient a reader more than jumping from subject to subject in a random manner. Subjects must lead on from one another and must be linked – more of this in the next chapter – but leading on from this is the idea of overall cohesion. It is possible to lead the reader smoothly through a set of topics which are unrelated, but the reader will be left with a dissatisfied feeling that things are not hanging together as they should. Consider the following:

- the sea shore is a habitat – *linked* via things that affect this habitat to

- humanity's effect upon the sea shore – *linked* via the things that people bring to the beach to

- picnic paraphernalia, swimming apparel and books – *linked* via people's reasons for using things to

- what people gain from books – *linked* via a specific example to

- the way children learn mathematical concepts from books – *linked* via comparing the ways adults and children learn to

- what an adult might gain from a particular book – *linked* via a specific example to

- an analysis of the novels of Charles Dickens.

The study of a natural habitat, mathematical concepts, the novels of Dickens – the links work well enough but there is no overall cohesion. What would the reader be expected to gain or to retain from this?

Obviously this is an extreme example but beware falling into this trap. You know your subject, you could leave out various sections without spoiling the flow for yourself because of your background knowledge.

You need to keep your readership in mind. For what level have you decided to write? Can you expect background knowledge? If so, how much? (See Chapter 1 for a fuller coverage of this particular aspect.) Does the overall plan hang together? A good check on both coherent flow and overall cohesion is the contents page.

COMPOSING THE CONTENTS PAGE

The contents page will come directly from your book plan. Do not be tempted to leave it until later if it proves troublesome. Trouble formulating the contents usually means problems with the plan. It is far easier to sort out problems of contents and ordering at an early stage. A contents list allows you to:

1.   Check the ordering of your topics. Do you cover the topic in one chapter and then explain some vital background in the next? Should the chapters be swapped? Is it okay to leave the detailed explanations until later or will it encroach upon your readers' understanding?

2.   See the overall picture. Do the sections within each chapter belong together? Do they flow properly from one to another?

Signs of potential problems

The topic that will not fit anywhere
This is topic which you consider vital but which seems to have no natural home in any of your chapters. Avoid the temptation to 'just bung it in here for now'. If you have several such topics, avoid also the temptation to put them all together in a chapter of their own.

Get to the root of the problem. Is the topic really vital? If so, then it must be vital to something else in the book. Find that something else and you are half way to finding the problem topic's home. Give real consideration to the question of whether or not a topic is essential. The fact that it doesn't seem to fit could be a sign that it is not.

The long diffuse chapter
This is not necessarily a problem. Some subjects, for example, lend themselves to a long and fairly diffuse coverage of background material. However, always look carefully at particularly long chapters, or chapters whose subheadings do not look especially cohesive.

- Will the reader lose his or her way halfway through? Think about splitting the material into more than one chapter.

- Are the topics genuinely non-cohesive? Think about re-ordering or moving specific topics out into other chapters to which they are more relevant.

Sometimes the problem is no more than ill thought out wording for the section headings. A contents list should not read like a list of unrelated items.

The very short chapter
Once again, this is not necessarily a problem but you should always have another look at a chapter which is very much shorter than all the others.

Has it been tagged on to cope with a troublesome topic that wouldn't fit anywhere else? If so, deal with the topic, as above.

To which other topics is it particularly relevant? Should it be in a chapter with them? Are there any other topics which should come out of other chapters to go with this one?

Clear structure
A contents list should give a clear idea of what is in the book. Use meaningful names for chapters and sections. A contents list is often used by potential readers before they buy. Compare the two examples in Figure 4 in terms of the information conveyed by each.

Consider the use of a consistent structure for chapter sections. Each chapter should have an opening section to introduce its topic and purpose and, if appropriate to link from previous chapters. Similarly, each chapter should have a concluding section to summarise the material and to link, if appropriate, to following chapters:

1. Chapter – name
2. Introduction
3. Body of chapter – sections as appropriate
4. Summary

1. Chapter 1

1.1. Introduction

1.2. Part I

1.3. Part II

1.4. Part III

1.5. Conclusion

1. Deciding the subject area

1.1. Introduction

1.2. Part I – Finding a gap in the market

1.3 Part II – Deciding the scope of the book

1.4 Part III – Writing a specific course book

1.5 Conclusion

Fig. 4. Using the contents list to best advantage.

Consistent naming of sections can give a good feel to a contents list – the feel of a well structured, well thought out text.

FORMULATING THE PREFACE

A preface should tell the reader in outline what the book is about and whether or not it is appropriate to him or her. The contents list gives a skeleton, the preface gives more detail on the scope, the depth and the philosophy of the text.

The preface should give information on:

- the aims and objectives of the book
- the intended readership.

A preface is also sometimes used to:

- give brief summaries of the chapters
- introduce particular notations used in the book.

In the preface, you should avoid:

- detailed explanations relevant to the subject matter
- detailed background material
- information that the readers will have to refer back to as they read the book.

A good guide is to make sure that the student reader working towards an exam would not have to revise anything in the preface.

CHECKLIST

- Write the contents list for your textbook.
- Using the ideas and results from previous checklists, write a preface for your textbook.

QUESTION AND ANSWER

I am finding it very difficult to write a concise preface and to identify readership groups. Does it really matter? It is only a peripheral part of the book after all.

The preface is vital, it describes the aims and objectives of the book as a whole. If you can't describe them, you won't achieve them. You must go back and think out your aims and objectives far more clearly.

CASE STUDIES

Amanda's aims are too narrow

'Just two comments' says Amanda's colleague, who has been reviewing her chapters for her as she writes them. 'Why don't you take this section further and cover the more advanced aspects? And here, why not give some more detailed examples, showing the different angles?'

'Well, I only cover that topic at a basic level in my course, so I didn't bother going any further with it. The same there really, I never go into that in much depth, so I've just given a flavour of it.'

'I see what you mean, but are you writing this book solely for your own course?'

'No, I'd like it to be of wider use.'

'Then you should think about a wider coverage, especially these areas that you're writing about anyway.'

Amanda nods thoughtfully. People teaching this very same course, she thinks to herself, will all put a slightly different slant and bias on the subject matter. If she takes account of this, she realises, she will increase her potential market.

Barry's aims are too wide

Barry formulates his contents page but it grows and grows. In the end he asks his supervisor for advice.

'I'm beginning to think,' he says, 'that I should be aiming for a much weightier book.'

'Theoretically, you could make a case,' his supervisor tells him. 'This subject could do with comprehensive coverage. But...'

'But you are going to advise against it.'

'Yes, I am. For one, this is your first book on the subject. You are not a well known author in the field. It's very unlikely that a publisher would risk the expense of a weighty tome. Secondly, think about the sort of books that are already published – the comprehensive coverage, the one everyone buys in a particular subject. The best of them, the really successful ones, have grown over time. They tend to be the second editions.'

'Back to the original outline then?'

'Yes, for now. Who knows though. If you stay in the field, if this book sells well... One day, you might re-write it and it'll become the classic in its field.'

Clare uses her knowledge of the field

'I heard you were up to the works the other day.'

'Yes,' says Clare. 'I was doing some research for my book.'

'What information can you find there you don't already have?'

'It's less the information than the audience,' Clare explains. 'I need to know what sort of people really need this book. Once I've identified them, I can work out which areas I need to cover in detail, how I need to bias the work.'

'Wouldn't it be more fun just to write it the way you want to?'

'Maybe, but I want it to sell. And to do that, I need to identify and cater for the people who need to know the subject.'

DISCUSSION POINTS

1. How important is the preface of a textbook to you when you are browsing with a view to buying?

2. Do you always skim through the contents list of textbooks you are thinking of buying?

3. When you are looking through textbooks in a shop or in a catalogue, what sorts of things attract you and why?

5
Structuring the Chapters

This chapter gives guidance on:

- getting the major aims across to the reader

- making the book a coherent whole

- effective exercises

- catering for the random reader.

STATING THE OBJECTIVES

Making it easy for the reader
Users of a textbook read to learn. It is your job as the writer, if you want your book to sell, to make your book one from which it is easy to learn. The text must not get in the way of the information. A textbook must be easy to read and present information in a way that is easy for the reader to retain.

A chapter needs to be:

- ordered – lead the reader smoothly from one idea to the next

- logical – always make it clear how and why the concepts and ideas are ordered

- themed – a chapter should have one underlying theme.

The objectives list
In a good textbook, there is no place for suspense. State your objectives and stick to them. The reader should start the chapter with a clear idea of what that chapter aims to do.

A concise list of objectives is often the best. It gives the reader, in nine or ten lines, a snapshot of the whole chapter. He or she knows what topics to expect and in which order to expect them. Needless to say, you should list the objectives in the same order in which they will be presented as the chapter develops.

Many textbooks will be presenting complex and difficult concepts. Good structuring of the material is an invaluable aid to assimilation.

There are various ways of stating the objectives, each equally valid in the right setting, for example:

- a numbered or bullet point list
- in a shaded box so that the objectives stand out from the rest of the chapter.

Label the objectives

Always tell the reader what is happening. If you are stating the objectives of the chapter, say so. Objectives lists can usefully be introduced by a word or phrase appropriate to the type and level of book being planned:

- Objectives
- The objectives of this chapter are...
- After reading this chapter, you will be able to...

The reader must be able to reach the end of the list without forgetting what was at the start. Go for **clarity** and **conciseness**.

LINKING THE CHAPTERS

Telling a coherent story

A textbook may not be a novel but it must tell a coherent story. A reader left wondering why he has jumped from one topic to another will become confused and find it harder to retain what he has read.

Sometimes it is obvious how one subject follows another, sometimes not, but do not leave the reader guessing. Link a chapter to the ones which precede and follow it so that the reader knows where he is and why.

Making the links

Linking one chapter to the next is not the only way to hold a textbook together. It is often necessary to mention a subject or a concept before it is explained in detail, or to refer back to it long after it has been explained. Make the link!

For linking explanations, concepts, sections, chapters and other texts use phrases such as:

- see section 4.2 for further detail
- as explained fully in Chapter 7
- as will be the subject of the next chapter
- as explained by A N Other in his paper/book....

Catering for the random reader

A textbook should not be written as though it will only be read sequentially. Bear in mind the reader who:

- may have read it all a year ago but who is now just dipping in to look up a particular topic

- is interested not in the major topic of the book but only in the material in a couple of chapters

- is evaluating the book for teaching purposes and who may start with the contents page and then jump to a late chapter to see how you have dealt with a particular aspect

- is a student opening the book at random wanting to know 'Will this book be of use to me?'

A section of text which talks about concepts without any explanation gives an unsatisfactory feel. However, you cannot give a full explanation every time you mention a topic.
    Compare:

> *The hypothetical house-builder, had he used Osbourne's model, would have avoided this problem.*

with

> *The hypothetical house-builder of chapter one, had he used Osbourne's model (see section 4.3), would have avoided this problem.*

In the first example, the random reader will have to go via the index for Osbourne's model and is unlikely to find the house-builder at all. By the time he has finished searching, he will be thinking that this book is hard work and will be looking along the shelves to see what else is on offer.

The average textbook reader is not reading for recreation. Textbooks are very often not read sequentially and the good textbook will make itself as accessible to the random reader as to the reader who goes through from beginning to end.

DEFINING THE TERMS

Keeping the reader on a firm footing

The definition of terms is all part and parcel of keeping the readers on a firm footing as they go through the book. A reader will be happier with the discussion of a complex concept if he is sure in his own mind of the underlying concepts.

Obviously, an advanced textbook must assume some existing knowledge, but even so, a clear and concise definition of the major terms used in a chapter can be of great help to the reader who is then:

• clear in his or her mind as to the precise meaning of the terms

• subconsciously tied into the subject matter of the chapter even more firmly

• able to devote him or herself to a deeper understanding of the subject matter.

For example, in *Software Maintenance: concepts and practice* (Takang and Grubb; ITP, 1996) one of the chapters deals with process models in a software maintenance environment. A section at the start of the chapter defines the terms *process, model* and *process model* both generally and as related to software. The chapter then develops into a detailed discussion of specific process models and their relevance.

Readers can easily assimilate the main thrust of the chapter because their memory has just been refreshed on the concepts which underlie it.

What to define

Terms like *process* and *model* are familiar but not everyone can immediately bring to mind a succinct definition for them either generally or in a particular context.

If the major terms used in a chapter:

- might be unfamiliar to the reader

- are open to several interpretations (most are!)

give serious consideration to a definitions section near the start of the chapter.

Glossaries
Glossaries are also useful and the defining of terms within the chapters does not obviate the need for a glossary. However, it is easier to be reminded of the exact definitions when and where you need them rather than having to flip forward or backward to a glossary.

REITERATING THE AIMS

Once the body of the chapter is written, you need to show that the chapter's objectives have been met. The body of the chapter will be appropriate to the subject matter and should mirror the stated objectives. The presentation of the material is an important aspect which is covered in a later chapter.

Reiterating the aims is a useful exercise. If you have difficulty in showing how the stated aims and objectives have been met, then they probably have not been, and some re-thinking is in order.

Remember the old adage:

say what you are going to say	the objectives list
say it	the body of the chapter
say what you have said	the summary

Linking the objectives to the summary
It is good practice to link your summary very precisely to the objectives list. A neat way of doing this is to use a summary list, one point per objective, to summarise how each objective has been met (see Figure 5).

Introducing the summary
Remember to tell the reader what is happening. If you are writing a summary list, then say so. Typical ways to introduce the summary include:

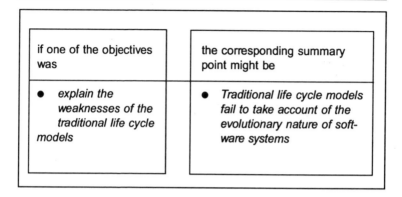

if one of the objectives was	the corresponding summary point might be
• *explain the weaknesses of the traditional life cycle models*	• *Traditional life cycle models fail to take account of the evolutionary nature of software systems*

Fig. 5. Linking objectives to summary.

- The key points that have been covered in this chapter are...

- Key points.

- Summary of major topics.

Note that the summary points will probably be longer than the objectives to which they relate.

The purpose of the summary is:

- to show how the objectives have been met

- to consolidate the main points of the chapter in the mind of the reader.

If readers go through a textbook reading only the objectives list, they should emerge with an overview of what the book aims to do. If on the other hand, they read only the summary lists, they should emerge with an overview of what the book has actually done.

WINDING UP A CHAPTER

Formally winding up

A chapter should be formally wound up. It should reach a tangible conclusion and it should be summarised. This is yet another device to let the reader know exactly where he is.

The concluding section, which may be only a paragraph, can come before or after the summary points as is appropriate to the particular subject.

The writing of the conclusion is a useful barometer for the writer. If you cannot write a clear and concise conclusion to a chapter, it is a sign that the material you are trying to conclude is inappropriate. Maybe you are putting too much into the chapter, maybe you are dealing with topics which should not be together.

Linking to the next chapter

Do not leave the readers in limbo at the end of a chapter. Lead them on to the next. The link paragraph is a useful device. It makes the forward path explicit:

- This chapter has done *this*.

- This obviously leads on to *that*.

- The next chapter will deal with *that*.

Or it can be used to show why the apparently obvious path is not being followed:

- This chapter has done *this*.

- This obviously leads on to *that*.

- But prior to dealing with *that* in detail, it is necessary to understand how *this* works.

- The next chapter will deal with *this*.

Always lead the readers through the text.
Do not leave them to find their own way.

STRUCTURING THE EXERCISES

What are exercises for?

Exercises give readers practice in the subject matter of the book. In doing them, they have to think out the concepts for themselves. Exercises both test and aid understanding.

Where to put the exercises

There are three general approaches:

1.   Put a number of exercises at the end of every chapter. This is

the most common.

2. Spread the exercises throughout the text.

3. Have a section for exercises apart from the main chapters. This is the least common.

To some extent the subject matter will decide which model is best to use. A good guide is to look through textbooks covering a similar field. See which models are used and which work best.

Exercises at the end of every chapter

Advantages

- gives an orderly list which is easily found

- gives the lecturer or teacher the opportunity to work through a full chapter and then set exercises

Disadvantages

- divorces specific exercises from the text to which they are especially relevant

- may encourage the student to skip the earlier exercises on the grounds that they have progressed beyond the early material

Exercises spread throughout the text

Advantages

- keeps the exercises with the text which is most relevant

- allows the student to stop and take stock as they work through the text

Disadvantages

- not so easy to locate as a list at the end of the chapter

- the student may skip the exercises in order to read the whole chapter first and then may not go back to them

Exercises together at the end of the book

Advantages

- easy to locate

- can be a useful format for the lecturer or teacher, for example when setting exam questions

Disadvantages

- means that exercises are located far from the text to which they apply

- makes it all too easy to ignore the whole section and do no exercises at all

Levels of difficulty

It is important to grade exercises. Teachers and students need exercises of different levels of difficulty to test their students' understanding.

There are three basic grades, with as many grey areas in between as you feel is appropriate to your subject.

The easy questions
These are saying:

- Did you read the relevant section?

- Did you understand what it was saying?

The expected answers more or less reproduce the relevant section of the text.

The more demanding questions
These ask:

- Have you read and understood the text?

- Can you apply it in a way related but not identical to the examples in the text?

The expected answers show an understanding of the text and also a general knowledge and understanding of the subject.

The advanced questions
These ask:

- Did you understand?

- Can you apply this knowledge to a situation beyond that described in the text?

Satisfactory answers to these questions require more effort. The mediocre student will be able to provide a satisfactory answer. The very good student will have the opportunity to shine.

CHECKLIST

- Identify five or six textbooks in a related field to yours and study the chapter structure. Note in particular how the reader is led from one topic to the next and list the good and bad points in the ways this is done.

- Pick one topic which is to be the main focus of one of the chapters in the body of your textbook. Think about how you will introduce this topic to the reader. List the salient points that you need to get across. From this list, create a list of objectives that the chapter must meet.

- Write the chapter structure – headings and subheadings – for the topic you have chosen. Consider how you will lead the reader from one area to the next. Have you got a logical and coherent flow? Compare your skeleton chapter with the objectives list. Has the bias of the chapter altered at all? Does the objectives list need to be modified. Will all the objectives be met?

QUESTION AND ANSWER

How do I decide which terms to define explicitly and which to assume that the reader already knows?

Give a sample of your work, without definitions, to a few people – to a group which is representative of your intended readership if possible. Ask them to read it and tell you with which terms they were or were not immediately familiar. This should give you a good indication. If in doubt, give the definition – better too many than too few.

CASE STUDIES

Amanda puts her course notes to good use
Amanda has decided to write the chapter of her book which is directly relevant to the part of the course she is currently teaching. She gathers together all the notes she has made over the years on this particular topic and goes through them.

'I've got this chapter written already,' she comments cheerfully to a colleague.

'What are your readers going to make of that?' he replies, pointing to a particular paragraph.

'Oh, I explain that in the lecture when I . . . . Oh yes, I see what you mean. I can't be on hand to explain my book to every reader. But still, I've learnt a lot about structuring notes over the years. I'm sure

I can put it to good use.'

Amanda is thinking positively about using her skills.

Barry can't get out of thesis mode

'Would you read this chapter and let me know what you think?' Barry asks his supervisor one morning.

Later in the day, his supervisor comes to him looking puzzled. 'I don't understand. Why are you dealing with this in so much detail? You barely mentioned it in your thesis outline.'

'Oh, it's not for my thesis,' replies Barry. 'It's for my book.'

'Go across to the library, Barry,' his supervisor says, tossing the chapter onto his desk. 'Get out two or three of the textbooks that helped you the most during your undergraduate years. Flick through them. Remind yourself why you thought they were good. Then come back and read this chapter again. Look at it through the eyes of an undergraduate.'

Barry does as he is told and sees the problem immediately. 'I'd never have waded through this,' he thinks. 'It's far too hard going. It doesn't give me any help at all.'

Barry has realised that writing for a thesis and writing for a textbook are two very different things.

Clare gives her reader too much to do

'I've written a chapter,' says Clare to an ex-workmate who has called round to see her. 'Would you give it the once over for me?'

'I'm really finding it quite hard to follow,' is the verdict, 'and I know the field. If I was new to the game, I wouldn't stand a chance.'

'But what's the matter?' asks Clare, surprised. 'I've split it into small sections specially to make it easy to follow.'

'But why have you split it the way you have? Here, for instance, why do you jump from this subject to that?'

'I needed to explain that first because I wanted to go on to expand this bit here.'

'Yes, I see that now, but it would have been a lot easier if I'd known at the time. Another thing, I didn't know where the chapter was heading until I was half way through.'

'I didn't want to say too early. I thought it would be confusing. I wanted to lead up to it gradually.'

'But it was more confusing not knowing where I was going. I couldn't see the wood for the trees.'

The criticisms continue and Clare begins to realise that she hasn't got the idea at all. She is learning that knowing the subject backwards is not, in itself, enough.

DISCUSSION POINTS

1. List general ways that text can be linked to create a flowing, coherent structure.

2. Which of these is especially relevant to your field?

3. What are the advantages, specific to your field, of an appropriately linked structure?

6
Writing the Beginning and End

This chapter gives guidance on:

- catching a reader's interest
- how to be positive at the start
- writing an upbeat finish.

CATCHING THE READER'S ATTENTION

The 'shop window' chapter
The introductory chapter is very much the shop window of the book. It sets:

- the tone
- the scene
- the level of the reader's expectation.

The introductory chapter needs to give:

- a snapshot of the book as a whole
- relevant background material.

A snapshot of the whole book
The more clearly a reader knows where he or she is in a textbook, the happier he or she will be with it. Use the introductory chapter to let the reader know exactly what the book is about.

Aim to give a clear overview of:

- the topics the book will cover
- how these topics are linked

- the depth and scope of the coverage

- the reasons for choosing this depth and scope.

Generally, textbooks range from very wide scope with little depth to very narrow scope with great depth.

Relevant background
The level of background material required before the textbook moves on to its primary focus will vary a great deal depending upon such things as:

- the level

- the scope

- the depth

- the intended market.

Background material can often fill several textbooks on its own and it is vital to keep the intended scope in mind when planning this aspect of the introductory material.

The amount of background material that you include can range from:

- everything in full to

- nothing at all.

Everything in full
This approach is appropriate to:

- basic texts which deal with very basic concepts as their main focus

- books of very narrow scope and great depth where the background material is
  - very specialised
  - absolutely vital
  - likely to be unfamiliar to the reader
  - not too lengthy.

Nothing at all
This approach is appropriate to:

- very basic texts where the main focus is at a very basic level

- books of very wide scope where relevant background material is better dealt with on a topic-by-topic basis throughout the book

- a book on a particular topic perhaps aimed very specifically at a particular course or where there is another book which is the special precursor.

Steering a middle course
The more usual way to treat background material is to steer a middle course somewhere between everything and nothing.
  For example:

- a reasonably full coverage of directly relevant material with an overview of and references to the more general background

- a concise overview, giving a framework of the whole area but little detail or depth.

Whichever approach you use, be sure to give comprehensive references. A reader may not wish to follow every reference given but there is a feeling of security in knowing that the references are there. References show that:

- the whole field has been covered, by links to other works if not explicitly in the text

- the route is open to find related material

- the author knows the field.

CREATING A POSITIVE OPENING

The snapshot view of the book plus the relevant background material will give the reader information on:

- what is in the book

- the particular slant with which the subject area is approached

- the depth and breadth of the coverage.

Over and above this, an important aspect of the introductory chapter is that it gives the feel of the book.

Aim to give the reader a positive feel and they will buy your book. The reader needs:

- a book he or she can read easily

- a book from which he or she can learn.

How to handle the introductory chapter

Do
- use the same overall style in this chapter as in all the others

- present the material logically and in order

- explain why topics are introduced in a particular order or a particular way.

Once again, this is all part of keeping the reader aware of exactly where he or she is. You tell the reader in overview at the start how you will deal with the subject and you reinforce this as the book progresses. Textbooks deal with complex issues and it is all too easy to lose the wood in the trees. A reader who is lost will have difficulty learning.

Do not
- present the reader with enormous amounts of detail

- present disparate areas without coherent links between them.

Too much detail is inappropriate in the introductory chapter. If it must go in, leave it until later.

If you find the introductory chapter dealing with a lot of disparate material which you find hard to link coherently, consider taking a step back. Present a more abstract overview in the introduction and put a background section into the relevant chapters. If this seems impossible to do, have a long and hard look at your book structure.

INSPIRING THE READER

Be positive in your opening and be enthusiastic.

Background material is not always easy to deal with and you may find yourself with a particular topic which you feel must be covered but which is rather tedious to write. Maybe it is a well established area with little academic challenge left in it, maybe it is tangential, but essential, to the main thrust of your book and is a topic which you find dull.

Beware of simply paraphrasing someone else's treatment of it just to get it out of the way.

If you are bored when you write the material, the reader will be bored when he or she reads it.

Useful alternative approaches

- Is there a different way of presenting the material, perhaps as a diagram (as in Figure 6)?

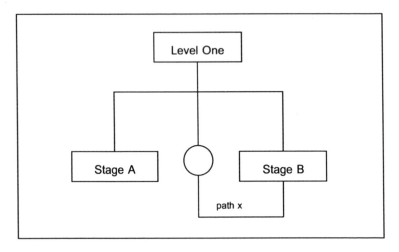

Fig. 6. Presenting information in diagrammatic form.

- Can you go back to the writings of the original pioneers in the field? Paraphrasing of words written when the field was new may give better results.

- Can you approach the topic by quoting from other sources? Why paraphrase a good, sharp quote into a tedious paragraph – use it as it is. Make sure that you attribute all quotes that you use.

PRODUCING AN UPBEAT FINISH

The main aim of the final chapter is to wind up the book satisfactorily. Do not leave the reader out on a limb.

A book dealing with one element of a large subject area is bound to leave much of the wider area uncovered, but do not leave the reader with the feeling that the book has left something out. You stated the book's aim and scope at the start. Reiterate this at the end.

- Show that the aims and objectives have been met.

- Leave the reader with the feeling that he or she has read a good, coherent and complete coverage of a particular topic.

- Make sure that all your loose ends are tied.

Onward and upward

All textbooks lead somewhere. Give the reader some pointers and leads:

- The book of narrow scope can give the reader pointers to the wider field.

- The book of wide scope can give the reader pointers to more in-depth treatment of certain aspects.

- The very basic coverage of a topic can give pointers to more advanced levels.

- Even the definitive coverage has somewhere to go. What are the areas of active research? What are the more intriguing of the currently unanswered research questions?

An upbeat finish serves to:

- inspire the reader to continue with the subject

- show that the subject area is alive and active

- give the reader a good feeling.

> *A good finish says 'it was worth your while to read this book and you have gained by doing so'.*

CHECKLIST

- Write notes on each of the following:
  - the overall scope of your book
  - the depth of coverage of the main areas
  - the general aims and objectives.

  Aim to be as concise as you can. These notes will become your introductory sections.

- List the areas of background material relevant to your book. Decide the level of detail with which you will need to cover each area and identify the areas which are relevant to the introductory chapter.

- Write a list of ideas for the final chapter. What slant will you use in summarising your book? What are the possibilities for ways forward that will give a positive feel to your final chapter?

QUESTIONS AND ANSWERS

My final chapter is much longer than the other chapters. Is this a problem?

Yes, usually it is. 'Final chapter' material often expands further than envisaged. Consider an extra chapter. A short and snappy final chapter is always worth going for.

My textbook is finished, but I have gone over the word count. Does it matter?

If you are a lot over, it probably does. Why have you gone over? Have you added extra material? Would it be a problem to edit out the extra length? Sort out the answers to these questions and then, before you do anything drastic to your manuscript, check with the publisher.

CASE STUDIES

Amanda doesn't change gear

'This gets easier,' Amanda tells a colleague. 'Once I'd made the decision to stick to a consistent format, the chapters started to flow nicely.'

The colleague, who has been reading Amanda's work for her as she writes, agrees that she has developed an agreeable and effective style.

'Here are the drafts for the first and last chapters for you to look at.'

'I'm not really happy with these chapters,' her colleague says later. 'They're not as good as the others.'

'What's the problem?' asks Amanda. 'I've been very careful to stick to the same style throughout.'

'I think that is the problem,' her colleague replies. 'There's a lot of stuff to learn in that first chapter.'

'Well, it is meant to be a textbook.'

'Yes, but I felt uncomfortable jumping into the middle of things too soon. I would have been happier with an opening chapter that set the scene for me. I came out of it with a lot of food for thought but no clear idea of where the book was taking me.'

'Yes, I see what you mean. It's a bit like an introductory lecture, setting the scene, telling the students what they should get out of the course, that sort of thing.' Her colleague nods agreement. 'And what about the finish? What was wrong with that?'

'More of the same in a way. I didn't want to end the book on a chapter just like all the others. I wanted something to round things up for me, to let me know what I'd achieved. Like the final lecture in a course where you summarise things for the students, remind them why they attended the course.'

Amanda is already making notes. The analogy with the lecture course has brought home to her the importance of the beginning and the end in the overall learning process.

Barry thinks big – too big! – but gets it right in the end

Barry goes to his supervisor for advice. He is depressed. 'It's this opening chapter,' he says. 'I don't know what to do with it. This is the structure so far.'

'So far!' says his supervisor incredulously. 'This chapter structure is probably longer than the whole chapter ought to be.'

'I know,' says Barry. 'But what can I do? I need to give the background before I can start.'

'Okay, let's have a closer look. Your ideas for outlining the aims of the book are fine.'

'Yes, I'm happy with that. I know what was helpful to me when I was an undergraduate.'

'But what about this? Anyone who didn't have a pretty clear idea about this side of things wouldn't be interested in your book, Barry, so why put it in at all?'

'But it's important background.'

'One sentence and a reference or two will be quite enough. Your readers don't want to plough through this level of detail. They'll have bought your book for its main subject matter. Now I agree that the next bit is important and you need to cover it in more detail, but not that much. State the conclusions, don't bother about the arguments that led up to them. Let the readers follow the references if they're interested. It's only the conclusions that are specifically needed for you to carry on and expand the subject.'

Barry nods. 'I see what you mean, but isn't it difficult to keep on track?'

'Don't look so down in the mouth, Barry, you're getting there and your final chapter is looking very promising.'

'Good, I was keen to give some pointers to more specific areas even though it's meant to be a general book.'

'Who knows, you might even inspire a few more into this research area.'

Barry goes away wiser and a little happier. He is learning the importance of keeping tight hold on the scope of the book.

Clare ties up her loose ends

'I want you to vet these drafts before I go any further,' Clare says to her friend. 'I know how important the start and finish can be and I'm afraid I may not have hit the right note.'

'The first chapter is excellent,' says her friend later. 'You've given a very clear overview and I feel that I know exactly where the book is going and what I'm going to get out of it.'

'I suppose it's not surprising that I got that right.' Clare says reflectively. 'After all, I wrote my first set of introductory notes over 30 years ago and I've been amending them ever since. But what about the ending. I couldn't really think how to slant it so I just went over things again the way I used to on the training courses.'

'I think it's worked well,' says her friend. 'It gives a timely view of the wider picture again. Your readers will have had to digest a lot of complex stuff by the time they get to the end. They'll be ready to have things put into perspective again.'

Clare has gained enormous experience over the years of how to teach and how to learn. She is using it to good advantage in her book.

DISCUSSION POINTS

1. What general background areas are relevant to your book?

2. Which of these would need to be covered in detail and why?

3. Which of these would you expect your readership to know already and in what depth?

7
Style and Presentation

This chapter gives guidance on:

- presenting the material in a way that makes it accessible to the reader
- signposting your text effectively
- deciding what system to use to present your final text.

BEARING IN MIND THE READER'S NEEDS

A textbook is read in a different way from a novel, a newspaper or a magazine. These tend to be read for relaxation, and readers don't need persuading or guiding through the text. A textbook is read in order to gather information or learn. In other words it is liable to be effortful reading, and one of your jobs as the writer of a textbook is to try to minimise the effort and make the book as attractive a read as possible.

Large blocks of text look uninviting. Short paragraphs with plenty of white space are much more inviting. Look at the two texts in Figure 7. Which one would you prefer to read?

Addressing the reader
How should you address your reader, and what tone should you adopt? Textbooks are usually formal in style for good reasons. The reader wants to feel that the writer is an authority or an expert, and a very informal tone would create the wrong impression, but you should not adopt a tone that is so formal that the reader is put off.

Markers of formality

Latinate vocabulary
Words that came into English from Latin tend to sound more

It is easy to confuse some bound morphemes that have an identical sound and structure. For example, English has free morphemes "hood" (a head covering) and "ship" (a sea going vessel). It also has the bound morphemes "-ship" and "-hood", that are both used to form nouns. "Hardship" means a state of deprivation or difficulty, "hard ship" means something different, a vessel that is difficult to sail, perhaps. "Motherhood" means the state of being a mother, not the head covering that a mother might wear. It is also easy to confuse part of a word that is a single morpheme, like "hammer", with a bound morpheme, in this case "-er", that is used to create nouns of agency (as in "play", "player") or adjectives of comparison or degree ("tall, taller"). Bound morphemes have two functions. One is to act as a grammatical marker, giving information about number, verb tense, aspect and other grammatical functions. These are INFLECTIONAL MORPHEMES. Examples in the data are -s, -ed, -er, (comparative) -es. The second is to form new words. These are called DERIVA-TIONAL MORPHEMES. Examples in the data are -un, -ly, -hood, -y, dis-, -ship, -er (to create a noun of agency).

It is easy to confuse some bound morphemes with the free morphemes that have an identical sound and structure. For example, English has free morphemes "hood" (a head covering) and "ship" (a sea going vessel). It also has the bound morphemes "-ship" and "hood", that are both used to form nouns. "Hardship" means a state of deprivation or difficulty, "hard ship" means something different, a vessel that is difficult to sail, perhaps. "Motherhood" means the state of being a mother, not the head covering that a mother might wear.

It is also easy to confuse part of a word that is a single morpheme, like "hammer", with a bound morpheme, in this case "-er", that is used to create nouns of agency (as in "play", "player") or adjectives of comparison or degree ('tall, taller').

Bound morphemes have two functions. One is to act as a grammatical marker, giving information about number, verb tense, aspect and other grammatical functions. These are INFLECTIONAL MORPHEMES. Examples in the data are -s, -ed, -er, (comparative) -es. The second is to form new words. These are called DERIVATIONAL MORPHEMES. Examples in the data are -un, -ly, -hood, -y, dis-, -ship, -er (to create a noun of agency).

Fig. 7. Using white space.

formal than words that came into English from other sources. For example, **ask** is Anglo-Saxon, **interrogate** is Latin; **climb** is Anglo-Saxon, **ascend** is Latin. You may find that Latin words make a text a bit too formal, and may be off-putting to readers.

Polysyllabic words
This can represent a major fault in textbook style. Sometimes you can't avoid long, polysyllabic words: for example, specialist terminology; but where you have a choice, go for the shorter, more familiar word. You are giving your reader a lot to cope with in the way of learning. Don't let your vocabulary be more obscure than absolutely essential.

Slang
It is best to avoid slang when you are writing a textbook. It gives an impression of a very informal approach, and slang 'dates' very quickly.

Complex sentences
Formal writing tends to use long, complex sentences with a lot of commas and semi-colons breaking the sentence up. Short, simple sentences are much better for delivering information. Don't make your reader work harder than necessary.

Passive verbs
Are you going to use structures such as 'Syntax is the study of principles and processes by which sentences are constructed in particular languages'; or 'Syntax is the study of principles and processes by which speakers construct sentences in particular languages.' The first sentence uses a passive verb that gives a much more formal tone to the text.

Impersonal tone
Passive verbs can give an impersonal tone as they tend to remove the writer from the text. Are you going to adopt a very formal, impersonal tone, or are you going to refer to yourself in the text and use *I* or *we*? Are you going to refer to the reader as *you*?

A highly formal tone is probably not the best tone to adopt. A less formal tone will make your book more accessible, though clearly you do not want to be too informal.

PRESENTING MATERIAL FOR LEARNING

Try to present the information in a way that makes it as easy as possible for the reader to follow, understand and absorb it. Give your reader a clear route through complex information. Start at the top and work your way down, or start at the bottom and work your way up.

Compare:

> *Sentences are the largest units of language with which this chapter will deal. Sentences contain phrases (see unit 3), phrases contain words (see unit 2) and words contain morphemes (see unit 1);*

with:

> *This chapter will look at sentences, phrases, words and morphemes. Sentences are the largest units of language and contain all the rest, and morphemes are the smallest units and don't contain anything. Phrases come in the middle and contain words, but don't contain sentences.*

Your readers need to be able to follow the subject through without having to backtrack because of the way the information is presented.

Experiment with different ways of presenting information.

- Lists can often be more useful than continuous prose.

- Information can be more accessible presented as a chart or a table.

Try not to make assumptions on presentation style based upon your own viewpoint. You are already an expert in this field. You are not a typical reader.

Look at textbooks that are considered successful in your area and learn from the way information is presented in these.

Try your material out on your intended audience. This is an essential part of the writing process. You will be able to gauge the success of your approach by the response it gets from your audience. Ask other people who are working in the field to trial sample chapters with their own groups.

Remember that you are familiar with the material and you know what your intention is. Can other people use it in a teaching situation, and do they find it useful?

SIGNPOSTING

A very important factor in making your book as accessible as possible is by signposting the text. This means just what it sounds like – giving clear indicators to the readers of where they are going, where they are now and where they have been. A well structured chapter will have clear signposting in the text (see Chapter 4), but there are other devices that can help to guide the reader through the text:

1. Number items in a list or use bullet points. These will help to clarify the points in a reader's mind.

2. Use sections and sub-sections to break material up into smaller, easy to follow chunks, and use clear headings.

3. Emphasise important words or points. When you are introducing a new term, make it stand out visually to warn the reader there is a new term coming up. Some books signal new terms or topics in the margin.

4. Use clear visual signals to indicate when you are coming to the end of a section or topic. If a reader is coping with a demanding piece of text, he or she will need regular breaks as the attention span tends to be shorter in these circumstances.

5. Present material in different ways. Give the reader's eye a break. Use figures and diagrams to clarify sections of continuous prose (and link figures and prose clearly in the text).

6. Use other devices to help make your text memorable. For example, cartoons can illustrate a point in a way that will help to fix it in the reader's mind, and at the same time give the reader a brief rest before moving on to the next point.

7. Make sure that quotes from other texts are clearly identified as such, and are clearly referenced, so your reader can look up the original text if necessary. Your publisher will have clear guidelines on this that you will need to follow.

8. Most importantly, *tell* your readers where they have been and where they are going to go next.

Remember:
say what you are going to say; say it; say that you've said it.

TO WORD PROCESS OR NOT TO WORD PROCESS

The simple answer is yes, use a word processor rather than a typewriter. Even if it means getting someone else to do it, or buying new software, or borrowing a computer, it will be worth it in terms of the ease of making changes and modifications.

Which word processor?

If there is a package with which you are happy and you do not feel comfortable about changing to something else then use that one. Computer whiz kids may tell you it is not state of the art but who cares? You are a textbook writer not a computer buff and if the package does the job then all well and good.

However, a word of caution, it can make life very much easier if you can swap electronic copy with your co-authors or with your publisher. In this case, packages which can read each other's formats are desirable. As a minimum requirement, make sure your word processor can export (and read) **ASCII** files.

Take care not to use something too complex. A big document is harder to handle than a small one and not all word processors will be able to handle a full book.

Microsoft Word is a good, widely used package, easy to get the hang of and fairly simple to use. Even this has complex features, however. Beware of being seduced into complexities that you cannot handle. If you are not *au fait* with things technological, ignore the more esoteric features but do try to incorporate the appropriate styles from the start. Get someone else to set up **style sheets** for you if you do not know how to do it.

Latex and similar systems (basically text with embedded commands) are useful only if you have experience. A small document is easy to write using *Latex* and gives impressive results when printed out. It also has the advantage that you can swap documents across computer systems and platforms without losing formatting. However, to produce a large document such as a textbook successfully – complete with diagrams, pictures etc – will inevitably need a degree of computer programming skill. If you don't have that to start with, leave well alone!

CHECKLIST

- Skim read a textbook in your area that you have previously identified as a good one. Analyse it by listing:
  a) General points:
  – Was it a good read?
  – Was it an easy read?
  – Was it nice to look at?
  b) Specific points:
  – What is the average number of sections per chapter?
  – What is the average number of illustrations per chapter?
  – Did the preface give good and clear aims and objectives?
  – Did the introductory chapter give a clear overview?
  – Was the final chapter upbeat?

- List all your options for word processors, and the advantages and disadvantages of each in time, money and effort.

QUESTION AND ANSWER

I've got the choice between my old word processor that isn't very sophisticated and a new one that is a lot more versatile, but I'm not too familiar with it. Which should I use?

This depends on the requirements of your book. If, for example, you need to index, or if you have a lot of references and footnotes then it is probably best to use the new one. You'll save a lot of time in the long run.

CASE STUDIES

Amanda thinks like a reader
'I just don't like this,' Amanda sighs, looking through her draft chapters. 'I don't know why. All the information is right, and I know these activities work well in class. I've used them.'

'Try it out,' suggests her colleague. 'Maybe you need a reader's point of view now.'

'Will you have a look at it?' Amanda asks.

'I think you'd do better trying it out on someone who might actually be using it. I'll ask one of my students to have a look.'

Two days later, Amanda's draft is back, and the student has given it the thumbs down. 'He says he couldn't read it,' her colleague reports. 'It was too difficult.'

Amanda can't understand this. She knows the text isn't too difficult. She looks at it again, trying to see it through a student's eyes. Then she has a brainwave. She goes back to her word processor and rearranges the text, using highlighting to pick out key words and terminology, bullet points to identify lists, makes the paragraphs shorter, and uses subheadings.

'I've rewritten that chapter,' she tells her colleague. 'Would your student have another look at it?'

'He really likes it now,' her colleague reports. 'He says you've made it much simpler and clearer now. I must say you did that rewriting quickly. I thought it would take you ages to simplify that lot.'

Amanda smiles to herself.

Barry falls apart

Barry is feeling good. He has his draft chapters completed, and now just needs one of his reviewers to try them out. 'I'm really getting the hang of this,' he tells his colleague, Dave, who has agreed to act as an informal reviewer. 'Let me know what you think.'

'I'm sorry,' Dave says, a few days later. 'I know you've put an awful lot of work into this, but the students found it hard to follow, and I found it difficult to help them, because, to be quite honest, I found it hard to follow as well.'

'Is it too difficult?' Barry asks, surprised.

'No, I don't think it's that. It just jumps around. One minute you're talking about one thing, the next you're talking about something else, and you haven't even said what you are talking about. You know where you are, because you've written it, but your readers don't.'

Feeling depressed, Barry wonders if he should give the whole thing up. 'Maybe I'm just not cut out to be a writer,' he says.

'Rubbish,' says Dave. 'You know you're really good at getting your ideas across when you are lecturing. Look at this chapter again, and pretend it's a lecture. Maybe you'll be able to see what's wrong with it.'

Barry has forgotten how important it is to signpost the text so that the reader can find his or her way through it. He has forgotten the first rule of clear signposting: say what you're going to say, say it, say that you've said it.

Clare forgets her audience

Clare is so involved with her textbook that she has even neglected to weed the garden. 'I've never really put everything I know about this down on paper before,' she says to her friend, Angie.

'It certainly looks impressive,' Angie says, looking over Clare's shoulder at her VDU. 'All those terms and initials! Do you really know what they all mean?'

'Of course I do.'

'What's this section about?'

'Well. It's all about the theory. It's about the ideas that underlie the theory in the book, and breaking it down into smaller units, and devising activities and tests. And about identifying your specific needs, of course. That's really important. Oh, and I'd better include . . . .'

Angie interrupts. 'That's quite some chapter. Let me read it when it's finished. I don't suppose I'll be able to understand it, though.'

After Angie has gone, Clare reads through her chapter. Then, with a sigh, she starts again. Clare has forgotten that she isn't writing for herself, she is writing for people who know a lot less about her subject than she does. Maybe she can turn her discarded chapter into an academic paper.

DISCUSSION POINTS

1. What do you like to see in the general appearance of a textbook?

2. What do you like to see in the general layout of a textbook page?

3. List some ideas for illustrations for your textbook.

8
Developing an
Academic Book Proposal

This chapter gives guidance on:

- identifying your potential market
- convincing a publisher of your viability as an author
- identifying appropriate reviewers for your book
- identifying competing publications.

RESEARCHING THE MARKET

If you are planning to write a book for the academic market, you will already be an expert in a particular field, and should be familiar with the important publications in your area. If you have carried out the research suggested in Chapter 1, you will be familiar with any gaps that exist in your potential market. It is important to make sure that you are up to date, because you are going to have to convince a publisher that your book is needed, and show how other books in the field don't do what your book will do.

SELLING YOURSELF

A publisher needs to know that:

1. **You can do what you say you will do**. If a publisher offers you a contract, he or she is taking a risk on your ability to deliver a suitable text to a suitable format on time.

2. **You have academic credibility**. For an academic book in particular, a publisher also needs to know that you have academic credibility. You don't need to be well known in your field (though it certainly helps if you are!), but you need to have a background that academics will respect. This is usually an

academic teaching or research background, but can also be recognised professional or vocational expertise.

> *If you can't convince a publisher that you can deliver a book that will sell, your proposal won't be accepted.*

The author's curriculum vitae (CV)

Your CV is your opportunity to sell yourself to a publisher. A CV for a book proposal may need a different focus from a CV for other purposes. You need to establish your academic, professional and vocational credentials, your previous publications (if any) and anything that will demonstrate that you can, and do, work reliably to deadlines.

The CV should tell the publisher clearly what your strengths are and why they are appropriate for this market. If you don't tell the publisher, he or she doesn't have the time to read between the lines of your CV and work it out. It is important that you identify your strengths so that you can produce a CV that will convince firstly your publisher and ultimately your readers.

Identifying your strengths

Your academic strengths are those things that give you **expertise** and **credibility** in the academic field. These will obviously include your qualifications, but can also include all other areas of your life in which you have gained genuine expertise in your field. Make a list of what you consider to be your academic credentials.

These should include:

- your qualifications, academic, vocational and professional

- your experience of working in the relevant field

- your experience in teaching or training in the relevant field at the relevant level

- your experience of research in the relevant field.

If you don't have at least two of these to include in your CV, you should ask yourself if the academic market is the right one for you. When people buy books in the academic field, they choose from publishers' catalogues, from reviews, and from reading the information on the book jacket, among other things. All of these

Subject area	Relevant experience
English Literature	writer of literary texts, theatrical or TV director or performer of literary texts
Education	experienced teacher or education manager
Social Sciences	experienced social worker, probation officer, community worker, community programme developer
Sciences	respected researcher, widely published research in reputable journals
Business Studies	management experience
Modern Languages	fluency, teacher

Fig. 8. Experience that will give you a good CV.

sources give information about the author and this is likely to influence the reader's decision about whether to buy or not.

Which of these author descriptions look best to you?

1. Joe Bloggs has a BA in communications from the University of Y.

2. Jane Bloggs has a BA in communications from the University of Y, and has taught English in schools for several years.

3. Jack Bloggs has worked in the field of journalism for many years. He trained as a junior reporter for the *Beighton Chronicle*. He has worked as a journalist for local and later national newspapers, and as a researcher and reporter for BBC radio. He currently teaches Journalism Studies at the University of Y.

4. Janet Bloggs has a degree in Communications from the University of Y. Her research includes work on exposure to the popular media and levels of literacy in young offenders. She currently teaches Communications Studies at the University of Z.

Clearly, authors three and four appear to have far better academic credentials than authors one and two, even though author three doesn't mention any academic qualifications. His combination of practical experience combined with his academic teaching makes him a credible writer in the field.

Author four has more traditional academic qualifications, with an interesting research background and teaching at a relevant level.

Generally, the kind of background that will impress your potential market depends very much on your academic area. Figure 8 shows some examples of the kinds of experience that would be relevant.

Your CV should also contain information about anything relating to the academic area that you have had published before. It doesn't matter if this is with a small publisher, a small circulation magazine or even your house journal. It is important because it shows that fellow professionals take you seriously, and are interested in what you have to say.

Is there anything else that you do outside of your workplace that might (creditably) bring your name to the attention of fellow academics and professionals? Are you an examiner in your field? Have you acted in an advisory capacity? Have you addressed conferences or meetings? Anything of this kind can add to your academic 'clout' and make you more attractive to a publisher.

Your CV is a tremendously important tool for getting a publisher to take you seriously in the academic field. Be careful you get it right.

Remember that there is no copyright on ideas. If a publisher is impressed by your idea but not by your CV, he or she could easily ask an established writer to take on the book.

IDENTIFYING REVIEWERS

The formal review process

Any proposal for an academic textbook will go through a process of review before it is accepted. It will also go through a process of review once it is complete. The initial proposal will probably be reviewed, and you will almost certainly be asked to produce a sample chapter or chapters. These will be sent to reviewers to comment on the content, the presentation and the potential market for the book.

Even if the reviews are good, you may be asked to amend your proposal in the light of the reviewers' comments, but if the reviews are poor, then your book may go no further, though by this stage you will have put in a lot of work. Clearly, you don't want your book to fail at this stage.

If there are genuine flaws in the proposal or sample chapters, then the review process will identify these. For minor flaws, this is a very useful procedure for you, the writer. It helps you to put a final polish on your ideas before you start to write the full text, and will, in the long run, produce a better book. Don't be discouraged if you are asked to adapt and rewrite. It means that the publisher has received generally favourable comments.

If you follow the process outlined in this book so far – identify an appropriate area, approach the right publisher, set a schedule that you can work to, design the framework of your book and your chapters appropriately – then the review process should not identify major flaws.

Who should review your book?

You need to know that your book has been reviewed by people who are expert in your area, and have some knowledge of the market you are targeting. The publisher, if he or she is experienced in this field, will have names of appropriate reviewers.

Remember, though, that you are the expert. If you are working in an overcrowded area, or if you feel that the possible reviewers may not be as familiar with the market as you are, then you may want to suggest reviewers to the publisher.

You will be familiar with many of the important writers, researchers and teachers in your field, and if you have had time to do the full research suggested earlier you will have a comprehensive list of names.

It is also possible that some experts in your field may not be sympathetic to the approach that you are taking. You may be proposing this book because you believe that the approach taken by other experts in the field is not appropriate to your market. If your book is reviewed by a writer of one of these books, he or she may well not be aware of the need for your approach. Again, identifying experts who are aware of this need will help your publisher find useful reviewers.

Ideally, your reviewers should have the following qualifications:

- expertise in your chosen field
- awareness of the area you are looking at
- experience of the needs of your target audience.

Informal reviews

Often your most valuable reviewers and critics are those people you see most often – your colleagues and friends. Their advice can be invaluable when it comes to identifying problems with your proposal and sample texts before the formal review process is started.

Colleagues are likely to have the professional expertise to comment knowledgeably on the content of your book. Friends can often give you useful feedback about style.

If you have friends or colleagues who are, or who are working with, your target audience, they can 'trial' your material for you to help you prepare it for a more formal review process.

COMPARING YOUR BOOK WITH RIVAL TEXTS

Your publisher will want to see clear evidence that you are familiar with potentially competing texts that are already on the market, and will ask you to identify these if you have not already done so.

Your initial research will have given you an overview of the market, but you need to look closely at existing textbooks that are apparently offering what your book is offering, and be prepared to put forward a convincing argument as to why your book addresses the needs of the market more effectively.

Make sure that you have checked the most recent bibliographies so you are familiar with the competition (see the Further Reading section).

CHECKLIST

- Write a short outline of your proposed book in no more than a page, giving:
  - main subject area
  - specific major aims
  - a paragraph explaining why no other book on the market fills this niche.

- Write your author's CV.

QUESTION AND ANSWER

Since the publisher is going to get this reviewed, is it important for me to get the proposal, the sample chapter and the rest of the book reviewed along the way?

Yes. These reviewers will spot things that you will miss, highlight problems you're not aware of, and offer solutions to problems you are having difficulties with. Also, a book that has been comprehensively tested on its target audience is always attractive to potential buyers if they plan to use it in a teaching capacity.

CASE STUDIES

Amanda finds her market

'You've seen my book proposal and my sample chapters, haven't you?' Amanda asks John.

'Yes, why?'

'I'm trying to sort out some market research to show my publisher. He thinks that the market may be a bit crowded for a new book. I'm sure he's wrong, but I don't know how to convince him.'

John looks at the notes Amanda has made on her visits to the library. 'What are these?'

'Rival texts, other publishers in the field, things like that.'

'Well, didn't you sort all this out earlier on?'

'I did when I was going to write for a specific course, but I thought that there was a wider market than that.'

'If you aren't writing for a specific course, then you aren't limited to the places that teach that course, are you?' says John.

'Of course!' Amanda is delighted. 'Why didn't I think of this before? This is just the sort of book they should be interested in in the US. And why not Australia? And Canada. There's a whole market out there I haven't even thought of.'

Barry sorts out his CV

Barry is looking through a box of floppy discs on the office filing cabinet. 'I know I put it somewhere,' he grumbles.

'What?' His research director is looking in the diary.

'My CV.'

'You aren't applying for another job!' He sounds surprised.

'No, it's for my book proposal. The publisher who is interested wants to see my CV. I've got it on disc, but I haven't needed it for ages. I've got all the other stuff together, so I just need to print off my CV and I can get it in the post for tonight.'

'Hang on a minute,' he says, 'if you haven't needed your CV for ages, is it up to date?'

'It is up to the time I started working here,' says Barry.

'But you've done a lot of important work in the field since then. I know this publisher. They want names that other people in the field will know. If you don't put all your research papers, and that international conference where you delivered a paper, they won't realise how many people know about your work.'

'You're right. On my old CV, I'm just another research student. I'm a lot more than that now. I'll bring it up to date. It can go in the post tomorrow. Thanks.'

Clare needs to sell herself.

'This is ridiculous!' rages Clare. 'My publisher doesn't like my CV! All that experience and he says I haven't got credibility!'

'That doesn't sound right,' says a friend. 'You've got plenty of expertise. Everyone in the business round here knows you.'

'Maybe that's the problem. I'm known locally, but not much more than that. And this publisher is looking for books he can sell overseas.'

'You don't have to be famous or anything though, do you?'

'No, but when people read about you on the book cover, they've got to feel that your experience and qualifications mean that your book will be authoritative, that you know what you are talking about. All I can say is that they know me well in Little-Binding-in-the-Marshes.'

'But look,' her friend says, 'you *do* have the expertise. You're just not showing how you got it in the right way on your CV. You talk about the company you worked for, but you have years of management experience, you organised training for people from a lot of other groups, and your training schemes have been used by a lot of other firms even if they didn't acknowledge it.'

Clare needs to sell herself to her publisher in a way that will convince him that her credentials will impress her potential market.

DISCUSSION POINTS

1. What are your major strengths?

2. Which of these are important to include in your publisher's CV and why?

3. How do your strengths relate specifically to the expertise you are using to write your textbook?

9
Maximising the Market

This chapter gives guidance on:

- recognising the needs of different markets
- targeting different markets
- giving your work a wider appeal.

WRITING FOR THE SCHOOL MARKET

Why do teachers use textbooks and why do schools buy books as resources for children?
Answer this question and you will help to make sure that your book is properly targeted at the school market.

Relevance to curriculum requirements and teacher needs
Teachers working in state schools work to very clearly defined curriculum requirements. The subjects contained in the National Curriculum at the time of writing are: English, Mathematics, Science, Design and Technology, Information Technology, History, Geography, Modern Foreign Languages, Art, Music and Physical Education.

If you plan to write for the school market and are not already familiar with the National Curriculum for your subject and target group, obtain a copy and make sure you know exactly what the requirements are. See the Further Reading and Useful Addresses sections for where to obtain National Curriculum documents.

Constraints on time and money mean that a textbook that offers a complete course in the relevant area of the National Curriculum for the year group will be a far more attractive option than one that will require the teacher to amend, add on and generally search through to identify areas that are not covered.

A good textbook for the school market will be designed to save the teacher time. The more time the teacher can spend teaching, the better. Textbooks that take over some of the burden of designing courses to deliver the curriculum, designing materials to deliver the curriculum, designing assessment techniques and programmes make excellent resources for schools and teachers.

Some publishing houses now specialise in producing photocopiable packs that contain aims, objectives, timed activities, suggested answers and materials. Not all teachers welcome such closely directed material as many prefer to develop their own materials and activities that suit the needs of individual classes, but these packs represent a valuable resource and are becoming increasingly popular.

Interesting and stimulating presentation, information and activities for children

Make sure that your book engages the interest of the children it is aimed at. The material should be:

- stimulating

- presented in a way that will appeal to your target age group

- relevant to them.

Use ideas and examples that relate to the interests and experience of your target audience. The activities should:

- be challenging and interesting

- help the children develop the knowledge and skills you intend.

Clear, well-structured development of skills

A good textbook for use in schools will progress through the subject clearly and logically, developing skills and knowledge in a hierarchical way. More advanced or complex skills and knowledge will be progressively introduced, and more basic skills revised as the book develops. The approach and breakdown of the subject will be clearly explained to the teacher in a preface or introduction.

Where appropriate, children will be told what skills they are going to develop or what they will learn, and they will be reminded at the end of each section of what they have learned. There will be opportunities for review and revision to allow individual children to progress through the book at their own pace, and to allow them and their teacher to check their progress.

Useful in a range of learning environments

There is no single successful way of teaching, and no single model of learning. Teachers use whole group teaching, small group work, individual teaching, 'chalk and talk', discovery learning. Learning takes place in classrooms, libraries and resource centres.

Which teaching and learning models are used for your target group? If you are not already involved in teaching, talk to teachers in a range of schools and centres, and find out which models are used. If you are a teacher working with your target group, make sure that you have a wider picture than just that of your own centre.

Does your book offer a range of teaching and learning models? The most useful textbooks for the school market allow for a variety of different activities and teaching and learning styles. Make sure that you offer opportunities for whole group learning, small group and pair work.

WRITING FOR FURTHER AND HIGHER EDUCATION

Further education (FE)

The FE market in Britain is expanding, offering education and training to post-16s in a range of different environments, including colleges, training centres and in the workplace. FE colleges are also moving into the traditional higher education (HE) market and, via franchising arrangements, offering courses to degree standard.

FE colleges and other centres operate under a funding system that is even more restrictive than that of schools. Flexibility, resource based learning (RBL), open learning and distance learning are all models that this market operates increasingly. There is also a developing movement towards telematics as a teaching and learning model.

As with the schools market, there is a range of teaching and learning models operating, and books that can be used flexibly to meet the needs of a wide range of students are more likely to be successful than more restricted texts.

Adapting your textbook to suit the needs of the market

There is still, and probably always will be, a role for the 'traditional' textbook in FE colleges. There is considerable cross-over with the schools market, with FE colleges offering the same courses as schools and sixth form colleges: GCSE, A-Level, GNVQ being common to both.

However, as traditional classroom time is reduced, the need is for resources that will deliver courses through more independent modes of study. Textbooks and materials designed to deliver a whole course via a distance or open learning mode are in increasing demand.

There is also a demand for materials for resource based learning designed to support work done in class or tutorial. This can be course-based (GCSE, GNVQ *etc*) or based on core skills: literacy, numeracy, IT, study skills.

Staff who teach in FE institutions have less and less time to prepare materials for course delivery. Books that can take some of the burden off the teacher are very welcome. Books targeted to deliver particular courses, with clear indicators in each section or unit to show what skill at what level is being developed, are what is required.

Remember financial constraints. A book designed to be used as a class set may not be expensive for one copy, but 20 copies will add up to a substantial sum. A photocopiable book may be expensive for one copy, but only one copy will be needed.

Writing for the HE market

This market is much wider than the schools and FE market, though sales of books in 'sets' are less likely. There is a far wider range of expertise in this market – academic undergraduate and post-graduate courses (*eg* traditional BA, some BSc, some BMedSci, taught MA), vocational undergraduate and post-graduate courses (*eg* speech therapy, teacher training).

The focus on learning in HE institutions is more individual. There is less demand in the teaching field for books that offer small group and class activities, and more demand for books that the student can use in independent learning.

WRITING FOR THE RESEARCH COMMUNITY

Why do researchers want to read textbooks?
Answer this question and you are heading towards the right bias and structure for a researchers' textbook.

General up-to-date information

Researchers who are starting out need general background information on their chosen area. They will need more in-depth information than they gleaned from their school or university courses and textbooks. A researchers' textbook starts at a higher level (the intended readership already know the general background) and continues right up to full treatments of the very latest in the field.

This means of course that your textbook must be regularly updated or risk becoming out of date. Remember however, that yesterday's researchers' textbook is today's undergraduate textbook and the school textbook of tomorrow.

Full explanations for complex research

When research projects produce complex and intricate results, they have to be made accessible to others, sometimes via textbooks in order that the work may be continued and used. It is usually those intimately involved with such research who write this type of book. Be sure to keep the distinction clear between explaining how the results were achieved and how to use the results.

Researchers wishing to verify the work and maybe continue it will want to know the minutiae of the means by which they were achieved – the compromises, the alternatives, the controversies. Those wishing to use the results will want clear explanations – what do the results mean, how should they be used, how do they work.

Talking to academia

Academia wants the whys and wherefores. How did these ideas originate? What are current opinions? How have opinions changed? Is there controversy and if so what is it? Researchers are looking to push back the boundaries of knowledge. To do that effectively, they need to know what is current and – often more importantly – why.

WRITING FOR INDUSTRY

Why does industry need textbooks?
Answer this question and you are heading towards the right bias and structure for a textbook for industry.

General up-to-date information

Good, well written and well researched textbooks are always useful – to get employees up to scratch in a specific field, or for potential employees to enhance their job prospects by increasing their knowledge. This type of book is often very specific to a narrow field and to a particular industry. Often the required information is contained in booklets and leaflets produced in-house. However, where the industry is large enough and where there is sufficient scope, a textbook is a real possibility and will have a captive market ready and eager to snap it up.

Specific information on complex subjects

Industry is not so concerned with the whys and wherefores. Industry wants to be able to make use of state of the art knowledge. How and why the algorithm developed is less important than how the algorithm works and how to implement it.

Find out exactly what level of knowledge is needed and write to that level. If you write to more than one level within the same book – and there is no reason not to – keep things separate. Suppose you want to write about a specific piece of research and describe exactly how it might be used as well as who will find it useful and why. The question of whether or not to use the work is a management decision. At this level, the finer detail of how the results are put to use is not relevant. The questions to answer are those along the lines of:

- Will this approach be effective?

- Is this a better way than the way we go now?

Once the decision has been made to go down a particular route, the questions then become:

- How can this be implemented?

- What is the most efficient way of doing this?

Do not mix the two. Use separate sections to describe the different levels. Those who are implementing the research do not want to have to wade through the underlying theory, they just want the instructions on how to do the job. Likewise, those assessing the area for suitability do not want to be presented with the detail of implementation.

> *Always look at what you write through the eyes*
> *of those who will need to use it.*

Talking to industry

Never lose sight of the fact that industries aim to do a particular job in order to make money. They will buy books which further this aim. Industry cannot do basic research. It cannot afford to. However, it is always eager to exploit research results and books showing exactly how to do this will find a market.

WRITING FOR AN INTERNATIONAL MARKET

Aiming specifically at the international market will involve specific research into your own subject area and the needs of the wider market. It is something that must be done with care. In targeting the international market, you are aiming to widen the audience for your textbook. Inadequate research, however, may lose you the home market.

If you are writing for examinable courses, then check up on overseas syllabuses. A very small addition or amendment to your textbook may increase your potential market enormously.

People like to *feel at home* in a textbook. Familiarity with the examples used helps understanding. A textbook which is overtly country-specific will be of less appeal in other countries.

> *Avoid being country-specific so that the textbook can apply in several countries but do not be so non-specific that it does not apply anywhere.*

A ploy that is used quite often is to employ one country (the one you know most about) as the major case study, but give comparative examples from other countries as well. This gives you the opportunity to write most about what you know best and a little research can give your textbook a satisfyingly international slant.

CHECKLIST

- Write a book proposal to the following format, using sections from previous checklists:
  - working title
  - the main subject area
  - outline of the potential market
  - brief details of the three most directly competitive titles, saying why your book is different
  - the names of two reviewers
  - an estimate of how long the book will take to complete
  - a short outline of the book, stating its major aims and objectives.

QUESTION AND ANSWER

I have planned my book in detail but now a new syllabus has come out. How should I deal with this?

Whatever you do, don't ignore it. Being out of step with the current syllabus will drastically cut your market. Everything in the new syllabus will be related to the old in one way or another, much of it may hardly have altered at all. Get to grips with the new syllabus and adapt your textbook. Conforming to the new syllabus will be an excellent selling point.

CASE STUDIES

Amanda gives no thought to marketing
'Good conference, was it?' Amanda asks her colleague.

'Yes, thanks. Excellent. I picked up a number of useful new books.'

'I don't suppose they were advertising mine.'

'No, they weren't actually. Which publisher was it?'

Amanda tells him. 'That's a pity,' he says, 'they were there, but no sign of your book.'

Amanda sighs. 'Yes, that *is* a pity. It would have generated a few advance sales.'

'Well, why don't you tell them? Let them know about the conference coming up next month. That should be a good one for your area.'

Amanda looks surprised. 'Can I do that? Surely they'll already have made up their minds what books they'll be pushing.'

'Of course you can. They are as keen as you are to sell books. The difference is that you are that bit keener to sell your own book. Push them a bit. Point out what a good opportunity it is.'

'But won't they mind? It's up to them surely?'

'I'm sure they won't mind. Especially if it leads to increased sales. Who's their marketing person?'

Amanda looks blank. 'I haven't a clue.'

'Well, get on the phone at once,' her colleague urges her. 'Get a name. Then pass on those conference details.'

Barry does his homework
'Can I re-schedule our meeting?' Barry asks his supervisor. 'I want to do some market research.'

'What kind of market research?'

'Get some addresses, names, relevant journals, academics active in the field, maybe a few commercial concerns.'

'What's all this for?'

'The publisher's rep mentioned ages ago that they'd be asking me for some ideas about where to advertise the book. She's ringing later, so I want to have the information ready.'

Later, Barry smiles as he takes down the name of his marketing contact. 'If you can contact him directly,' the publisher's rep concludes, 'with any ideas you might have – conferences, journals and so on – he'll make sure that your book is advertised to best effect.'

Barry puts the phone down, affixes a stamp to the newly addressed envelope and drops a comprehensive list in the post.

Clare assumes it is up to the publisher

'The publishers have asked me to suggest places where the book should be advertised,' Clare tells a friend.

'Why do you sound so surprised?'

'Well surely that's up to them. What do I know about advertising books?'

'OK, just for fun then, tell me where you would advertise it.'

Clare considers, 'The usual journals I suppose, then I'd write to the major people in the industry.'

'You'd know who they were, I suppose?'

'Yes, of course. I was in the industry for decades.'

'And how on earth do you expect the publishers, who certainly haven't been in the industry for decades, to have a clue?'

'Isn't that their job?'

'What, to get to know the specialist fields of every textbook they publish? Their job is to publish books.'

'Yes, I see what you mean,' says Clare. 'I just hadn't thought it through before.' She sits down and begins to draft a list.

DISCUSSION POINTS

1. In which of the potential markets outlined in this chapter do you feel most at home and why?

2. What areas of your expertise are most likely to appeal to an international market?

3. In what way would your expertise appeal to the home market?

10
Starting from the Academic Paper

This chapter gives guidance on:

- making the transition from academic paper writing to textbook writing

- the difference between academic papers and textbooks in terms of priorities and potential markets.

Many textbooks spring from the writing of academic papers, and this chapter looks briefly at the structure of the academic paper as opposed to the textbook. A common problem – and cause of much heartache and re-writing – is a failure to swap from 'academic paper mode' to 'textbook mode'.

KNOWING YOUR SUBJECT

The textbook writer needs to know his or her subject just as well as the writer of quality academic papers. But there are differences in the levels of knowledge. The writer of an academic paper is often looking in depth at a very small part of a wider field. The textbook writer will usually have to explore the wider field as well as the specific focus of the book.

The focus of a textbook tends to be wider anyway than the focus of an academic paper which may be a report on a single experiment. Anyone aspiring to write a comprehensive work will almost inevitably find coverage is required of areas which are not his or her own specific field. You would not do that when aiming to produce a quality academic paper.

However, the coverage of these peripheral areas is important. It is not after all a case of becoming an expert, or of doing original research. It is a case of studying what has been done in the field and reporting it – basic research work in other words, and something at which a seasoned academic paper writer should be very good.

EXPLORING YOUR MARKET

For those wishing to write a textbook who have already established themselves as authors of academic papers, there are a number of points to consider regarding the respective markets.

The market for academic papers is much more focused in the sense that a particular journal will have a specific focus from which it is unlikely to deviate. Knowing the specific market is vital in targeting academic papers.

By and large, what you write and the way you write it is decided by the journal at which you aim: the subject matter, the bias, the length and the structure. Textbooks are different. You know the particular needs of the market. You may be writing a book to support a course that you teach, in which case you know best how it should be structured and how it should be focused. You will need to do some research on the wider market – you need to know what will give this book appeal beyond your course, your curriculum, your level or your country.

Where to start

A good track record with academic papers is a good starting point for textbook writing. It is an authentic indication that you know your subject.

Academic papers are good source material for textbook writers in more ways than one. The papers themselves obviously contain valuable information but you can also take advantage of the contacts to be made. If you come across a particularly relevant paper and would like to know more, you can usually contact the writer fairly easily. Conferences are also a good source of contacts, and a useful means of getting the feeling for an area, where information is needed, where the gaps are in the market.

Make special use of international conferences to find out what is available and what is lacking on the international market. Look out for opportunities to team up with another author with complementary knowledge.

STRUCTURING THE PAPER

Journals vary in their requirements for structure of the papers they publish. It is vital that you get the relevant author guidelines before you start. In general, the required structure will follow the usual format:

Say what you are going to say.
Say it.
Say what you have said.

Figure 9 gives a rough guide to the minimal structure.

Header (title, author details and date)

Abstract

Keywords

Introduction

Body

Conclusion

References

Fig. 9. Minimal structure for an academic paper.

See the Further Reading section for where to find detailed advice on the writing of academic papers.

RECOGNISING THE PRIORITIES

Textbooks and academic papers differ in very basic ways. It is important to recognise the differences in order to make the transition from academic paper writing to textbook writing.

An academic paper is a scientific report on work done, on theories propounded, on experiments; it is aimed at those with a specific academic interest, it is a bald and formal statement of fact. It does not need, and indeed should not have, many of the things a good textbook needs. For example, an academic paper is aimed at a community who already knows the field, it does not therefore need the wide background coverage that will be necessary in many textbooks. A priority in a textbook is the accessibility of the information within it for the target readers – those needing to learn. This is not to say that an academic paper should be badly written and give no thought to readability, but far fewer concessions will be made in an academic paper to those unfamiliar with the territory.

There are also important areas in common. For example, the need for a clear statement of purpose and the need for cohesion and structure.

The priorities are different and in order to make the switch and put your knowledge in textbook format when you have been used to writing academic papers, you need to recognise these.

Changing priorities

Academic papers
- Have a more formal and rigid style.

- Lay great emphasis on getting the facts down. This may mean long blocks of text.

- Need comprehensive but terse referencing. The reader is left to look things up for him or herself.

- Are ordered. The reader is expected to read through from start to finish. No concession is made to the reader just dipping in.

- Are often packed with detailed information, for example, full tables of results.

- Have no 'frills'. Diagrams and tables are used to communicate information, rather than to clarify what is already in the text.

- Are very focused. Deciding what does and does not belong in a particular paper is not usually a problem.

Textbooks
- Have a more accessible style.

- Should take pains to make the facts palatable, for example by avoiding long blocks of text.

- Need comprehensive referencing, but will include explicit links. The situation where the reader has to go and read some other publication in order to understand a topic should be avoided.

- Make allowance for the random reader, make it as easy as possible to use the book as a reference to be dipped into. This makes the book more useful and therefore more saleable.

- Often avoid complete information. For example, long and

detailed experimental results will be summarised rather than given in full. Readability is a priority.

- Abound with 'frills'. Diagrams will be used to clarify information already given in the text. Anything which aids the reader's retention of the subject matter is useful. You will find far more textbooks than academic papers containing cartoons, for example.

- Will have wider aims and objectives.

CHECKLIST

- Choose a publisher from the list you wrote for Chapter 2, contact them and discuss your idea for a textbook. Use the short outline you wrote for Chapter 8. Say that you would like to submit a book proposal and ask them to send you a proposal form.

- Complete the proposal form when it arrives. Most, if not all the material you will need will be ready from the work you have done for Chapters 1 to 9.

QUESTION AND ANSWER

A colleague who wrote a textbook last year received five per cent more royalties than I am being offered. Can I ask for more?

By all means. But do weigh up the pros and cons. Your publisher may be offering a wider market. Standard royalty deals do differ between the arts and the sciences and between publishers. The smaller publishers in particular may be prepared to negotiate on royalties, some will even suggest profit sharing agreements, but beware – with royalties, you get something for every copy sold; in a profit sharing deal you may not get anything at all if the book doesn't sell well.

CASE STUDIES

Amanda enhances her career prospects
'I thought you'd finished with all that,' Amanda's colleague indicates the pile of journals at her side.

   'Oh, the book's finished but I'm putting together a paper for this journal.'

'Why? Haven't you got enough to do?'

'Plenty,' Amanda laughs, 'but the thing is that writing the textbook brought it home to me that I know a great deal about the subject area. I have things to contribute to the current debate.'

'And with a string of up-to-date publications in the journals,' her colleague continues, 'you stand a far better chance in the job and promotion market.'

'Exactly,' Amanda nods and returns to her work.

Barry interlinks his writing skills

'This draft is very good, Barry,' says his supervisor. 'It's almost ready to send off.'

'You sound surprised,' says Barry, a little taken aback.

'Well, I have to confess that I am a little. I have no complaints about your work but always in the past I've had to make some fairly radical suggestions for modifications in the way you present it.'

Barry considers. 'Do you mean it's more readable than usual?'

His supervisor nods. 'And something else, you've already sussed out the house rules for format, length and so on. I'm used to reminding you about all that.'

'I thought so,' Barry looks smug. 'It's the book. It's taught me about writing, especially to make things easier for the reader to understand. I know I'm writing for an audience of experts, but it occurred to me that that's no reason to make the paper turgid and hard to read. As for house rules,' he laughs, 'I've learnt my lesson there. After all I had to go through to get the book into shape, when I could have had it all done if only I'd taken account of it from the start...'

Clare widens her horizons

'How do you feel having finished the book?'

'Nothing at all like I expected to feel,' Clare replies.

'You said you expected to either feel satisfied at a job well done or rather empty at suddenly having nothing left to do.'

'It's odd, Clare muses, 'I do feel satisfaction of course, but I don't feel that the job *is* done.'

'What do you mean?'

'There's more to do. Researching the book has given me a much deeper understanding of the issues. I've been able to get to grips with the whole area in a way I never had time for when I was working full-time.'

'You're not going to start another book, are you?'

'Oh no, I haven't got nearly enough material to do that – yet. But I do feel that I have things to offer. I'm putting some of my findings together into a paper. Who knows, I might be a regular on the conference circuit from now on!'

DISCUSSION POINTS

1. What are the major international journals in your academic area?

2. Which journals do you read regularly?

3. Which journals would you like to write for, and why?

AND FINALLY...

If you have followed the suggestions from the checklists, and given thought to the discussion points, you already have most if not all of a textbook proposal. If you have been realistic in your choice of subject area and have done your homework in your choice of publisher, then there is no reason why a book contract shouldn't follow very soon.

Once you have your contract, don't let the writing process become too painful. Take note of the advice given on timetabling and scheduling. Use *this* book as a textbook and keep coming back to it as your book takes shape. Let the advice given here ease the operational and bureaucratic load. Allow yourself to enjoy the fun bit – the creativity of actually writing your own textbook.

Good luck!

Glossary

A-Level. Advanced level – a post-16 qualification used in large parts of the UK.

AS-Level. Advanced Supplementary level – a qualification currently offering the same standard as A-Level but across a narrower field. Generally equivalent to half an A-Level.

ASCII. American Standard Code for Information Interchange: a character set (including upper and lower case letters, digits and punctuation) with a pre-defined computer-friendly format understandable to most computers and computer languages.

BA. Bachelor of Arts degree: advanced level qualification in the Arts, Humanities or Social Sciences available in universities, colleges of higher education and through open learning.

BSc. Bachelor of Science degree: advanced level qualification in the Sciences available in universities, colleges of higher education and through open learning.

Core skills. Skills in English, numeracy, communications and IT. Sometimes called **Key Skills**.

Curriculum. The outline of a course giving a brief indication of its subject contents and level.

CV. Curriculum vitae: an account of your career and skills. A useful tool in selling yourself as a potential writer.

GCSE. General Certificate of Secondary Education: a qualification taken by most people in English and Welsh schools at the age of 16.

GNVQ. General National Vocational Qualification: a vocational qualification available at GCSE and A-Level equivalent.

Latex. A document processing system designed to produce high quality typesetting which allows the use a high degree of flexibility. It is not a WYSIWYG (qv) system. The text is converted to its finished format by a special computer program. Very useful for complex technical documents with a lot of mathematical symbols, but not recommended for the novice user.

Microsoft Word. A widely used WYSIWYG word processing package which runs on either a PC or a Macintosh computer.

National Curriculum. The curriculum applying to pupils of compulsory school age in maintained schools. The National Curriculum document outlines programmes of study and attainment targets.

NVQ. National Vocational Qualification: a vocational qualification integrated into industry and commerce.

SATs. Standard Assessment Tests: national tests taken at specific key stages in pre-16 education.

Style sheets. Electronic templates which can store such things as specific formatting for headings and text. Once set up to the required specifications, the documents created using these templates will already adhere to the necessary house rules for text formatting, spacing, font size *etc*.

Syllabus. The programme of a course of study.

WYSIWYG. What You See Is What You Get.

Useful Addresses

Use the Year Books given in the Further Reading section to find the publishers relevant to your field.

CURRICULUM AND EDUCATION BODIES

Curriculum and Assessment Authority for Wales (ACAC), Castle Buidings, Womanby Street, Cardiff CF1 9FX.

Further Education Development Agency (FEDA), Citadel Place, Tinworth Street, London SE11 5EH.

Northern Ireland Council for the Curriculum, Examination and Assessment (NICCEA), Beechill House, 42 Beechill Road, Belfast BT8 4RS.

Office for Standards in Education, Alexandra House, 29–33 Kingsway, London WC2B 6SE (National Curriculum documents are obtainable from this office).

School Curriculum and Assessment Authority (SCAA), Newcombe House, 45 Notting Hill Gate, London W11 3JB.

Scottish Consultative Council on the Curriculum (Scottish CCC), Gardyne Road, Broughty Ferry, Dundee DD5 1NY.

UCAS, PO Box 28, Cheltenham, Gloucester GL50 3SA.

INTERNATIONAL CONTACTS

The British Council, 10 Spring Gardens, London SW1A 2BN.

The Commonwealth Institute, Kensington High Street, London W8 6NQ.

International Baccalaureate Organisation, 15 Route des Morillons, 1218 Grand-Saconnex/Geneva, Switzerland.

See also the Year Books of the Further Reading section.

EXAMINING BOARDS

Associated Examining Board/Southern Examining Board, Stag Hill House, Guildford, Surrey GU2 5XJ.

BTEC, Central House, Upper Woburn Place, London WC1H 0HH.

City and Guilds of London, 1 Giltspur Street, London EC1A 9DD.

Northern Examination and Assessment Board, Devas Street, Manchester M15 6EX.

Oxford and Cambridge Schools Examination Board, Purbeck House, Purbeck Road, Cambridge CB2.

RSA, Westwood Way, Coventry CV4 8HS.

Scottish Examination Board, Ironmills Road, Dalkeith, Midlothian EH22 1LE.

SCOTVEC (Scottish Vocational Education Council), Hanover House, 24 Douglas Street, Glasgow.

University of Cambridge Local Examinations Syndicate/Midland Examining Group, Syndicate Buildings, 1 Hills Road, Cambridge CB1 2EU.

University of London Examination and Assessment Council, Stewart House, 32 Russell Square, London WC1B 5DN.

Welsh Joint Education Committee, 245 Western Avenue, Cardiff CF5 2YX.

SMALL PUBLISHERS

There is no fully comprehensive list of small publishers. Your best bet is to contact the professional organisation for your subject area and ask if they keep a list. Small publishers do appear in the Year Books, but look also for contacts on information flyers, sent perhaps to local schools and colleges or available from the library.

THE INTERNET

These days, an excellent source of up-to-date information is the Internet. A great advantage of using the Internet is that you can conduct a fairly wide-ranging search, for example:

'Education in England and Wales'
and then refine it:

'Chemistry' or 'English Literature'
as much as you want:

'undergraduate', 'primary level', 'special needs'.

A multitude of sites are accessible and more are becoming available all the time. Examples below show the results of just a few searches:

Education – USA

Alabama education on-line – http://alaweb.asc.edu/ed_dir/education.html

Boise state university home page – http://www.idbsu.edu/

University of Alaska Anchorage – http://orion.alaska.edu/

University of Arizona – http://www.arizona.edu/

University of Delaware – http://www.udel.edu/

University of Florida's home page – http://www.ufl.edu/

University of Hawaii Information Technology services – http://www.hawaii.edu/uhinfo.html

Yale University – http://www.yale.edu

International Foundation for Gender Education (IFGE) Resource Guide USA – http://www.transgender.org/tg/ifge/states.html

USA2100 Computer Learning Centre – http://www.usa2100.org/

Southeast Regional Climate Center – Education Center – http://water.dnr.state.sc.us/climate/sercc/

Home Education Resources Center (HERC) – http://www.cts.com/~netsales/herc/

StarkNet Boundary Breakers: The Boundary Breakers are a group of teachers from several school districts in Stark County, Ohio, USA, committed to the idea of 'classrooms without walls.' – http://jasper.stark.k12.oh.us/gopher://199.218.193.6/1

Education – Australia

University of Western Australia – gopher://uniwa.uwa.edu.au/

Queensland Department of Education Virtual Library – http://cooroomba.client.uq.edu.au/

The Australian National University – The International Education Office – http://online.anu.edu.au/ieo

The National Library of Australia – http://www.nla.gov.au/

Graduate School of Management – Macquarie University, Australia – gopher://gsmgopher.gsm.mq.edu.au/

Deakin University, Australia – http://www.deakin.edu.au/

WWW Archive for Electric Power Engineering Education – http://www.uow.edu.au/pwrsysed/

Architecture and Fine Arts – University of Western Australia – http://www.arts.uwa.edu.au/ArchWWW/ArchitectHome.html

MONASH: Australia's International University – http://www.rdt.monash.edu.au/

Guide to Australia – http://www.csu.edu.au/education/australia.html

The Australian National University – The International Education Office – http://online.anu.edu.au/ieo

Studyabroad.com – http://www.studyabroad.com

Queensland Department of Education Virtual Library – http://coroomba.client.uq.edu.au/

The National Library of Australia – http://www.nla.gov.au/

The Australia National University Index of Australian Libraries – http://info.anu.edu.au/ozlib/ozlib.html

Information Libraries Access Network (ILANET) – http://dixson.slnsw.gov.au/

Education – New Zealand

New Zealand Government Online Blue Pages – http://www.gwr.govt.nz/

Education – Singapore

The National University of Singapore – gopher://nuscc.nus.sg/

Nanyang Technological University – Business School – http://www.ntu.ac.sg/nbs/index.shtml

Education – Canada

Royal Military College of Canada Department of Mathematics and Computer Science – http://ma1.rmc.ca/

Acadia University's Continuing Education Home Page – http://webster.acadiau.ca/conted/

University of Western Ontario – Western Business School (Canada) – http://www.business.uwo.ca/

Education – Middle East

Lis-middle-east is an electronic mailing list that deals with concerns common to librarians, archivists and academics with responsibility for, or an interest in, Middle Eastern and Islamic collections and bibliographies.

Mailing list: mailbase@mailbase.ac.uk

Kuwait University – http://www.kuniv.edu.kw/

Education – India

Birla Institute of Technology, Mesra, Ranchi, INDIA – http://www.mgmt.purdue.edu/MIS/BIT/bit.html

Dr. Ambedkar Institute of Technology (at Bangalore University,

Bangalore, INDIA) – http://www.acsu.buffalo.edu/~gadi/drait/
Government College of Techology, Coambitore, Tamilnadu,
    INDIA – http://web.mit.edu/naren/www/gct/GCThome.html
Alagappa Chettiar College of Engineering and Technology – http://
    www.ems.psu.edu/~narayan/ACCET/

Continuing education (as a sub search of Education – UK)
Continuing-education is an electronic mailing list for discussions
    and the dissemination of information regarding continuing
    education in higher education.
Mailing list: mailbase@mailbase.ac.uk

Science-education (as a sub search of Education – UK)
Review: The science-education mailing list provides a forum for
    academics engaged in the study of science education. The list
    focuses on practical and theoretical issues relating to the teaching
    of science and the professional development.
Mailing list: mailbase@mailbase.ac.uk

Further Reading

There is an enormous number of books on education systems in general and also about specific areas. It is your own subject area and proposed treatment of it that dictates which are the most useful to you. The further reading below gives a sample of texts which show the diversity available.

YEAR BOOKS

Writers' & Artists' Yearbook (A&C Black).
The Writer's Handbook (Macmillan Reference Books).
Changing Populations Changing Schools, Chicago, Illinois. Yearbook of the National Society for the Study of Education Pt. II. (University of Chicago Press).
The World of Learning (Europa Publications, 1996).

LIST OF BOOKS IN PRINT

Whitaker's British Books in Print is the most useful list of British books. Many libraries will have this publication available on CD-ROM which greatly facilitates the task of searching through it.

WRITING ACADEMIC PAPERS

How to Write and Publish a Scientific Paper, Robert Day (Cambridge University Press, 1994).
Handbook for Technical Writing, James Shelton (NTC Business Books, 1994).
A Manual for Writers of Research Papers, Theses and Dissertations, Kate Turabian (Heinemann, 1982).
MLA Handbook for Writers of Research Papers, Theses and Dissertations, Joseph Gibaldi and Walter Achtert (Modern Language Association of America, USA, 1984).

GENERAL NON-FICTION WRITING

Writing a Non Fiction Book, Norman Toulson (How To Books, 1996).

Writing Non-fiction, Diana Bentley and Dee Reid (Scholastic Publications, 1995).

Writing Creative Non-fiction, Theodore Cheney (Ten Speed Publ. USA, 1991).

EDUCATION AND TRAINING IN THE UK

The Education Authorities Directory (School Government Publishing Ltd).

Review of Qualifications for 16–19 year olds, Ron Dearing. March 1996. SCAA Ref: COM/96/459.

Individual syllabuses – see the Useful Addresses section for where to obtain these.

The Role of the Company in Generating Skills: the Learning Effects of Work Organization United Kingdom, Kenneth Walsh, Andy Green and Hilary Steedman. European Centre for the Development of Vocational Education (Luxembourg Office for Official Publications, 1996).

A British 'Baccalaureate' Ending the Division between Education and Training, David Finegold (Institute for Public Policy Research, 1990).

Reform of Post-16 Education and Training in England and Wales, William Richardson, John Woolhouse and David Finegold (eds) (Harlow Longman, 1992).

THE EDUCATION SYSTEMS OF DIFFERENT COUNTRIES

An excellent source of information on education systems is the Internet – see the Useful Addresses section for details.

The National Curriculum – see the Useful Addresses section for where to obtain documents pertaining to the UK National Curriculum.

A comprehensive bibliography export of education services and Australia full-fee policy for overseas students, Don Smart and Grace Ang. Working papers; no. 9. (Murdoch University, Asia Research Centre, 1992).

Creativity Across the Curriculum, Classroom and Curriculum in Australia, no. 3, Millicent Poole (Allen and Unwin, 1980).

Developing Students' Library Research Skills, Bruce Christine (Higher Education Research and Development Society of Australia, 1992).

Adult Education in Australia, Derek Whitelock (ed). (Pergamon Press, 1970).

Adult Literacy Provision in Australia – Trends and Needs, Darryl Dymock (Australian Council for Adult Literacy, 1982).

Building for School and Community, 4 England, Australia (Organisation for Economic Cooperation and Development (OECD). Programme on Educational Building 1979).

Classification of Educational Systems. Australia. Luxembourg. Switzerland. (OECD, 1975).

Education in Australia, Phillip E Jones (David & Charles, 1974).

Decision-making in 14 OECD Education Systems (OECD, 1995).

Key Education Statistics [Singapore] (Singapore Ministry of Education, Education Statistics Section, 1981).

Reshaping local worlds formal education and cultural change in rural Southeast Asia, Charles F Keyes (ed) (Yale University Southeast Asia Studies, 1991).

Review of Government-funded Educational Research and Development in Europe, Sheila M Stoney, Fiona Johnson and Simon Gallacher. (National Foundation for Educational Research, 1995).

School provision for children of occupational travellers: report on the implementation of measures planned by the Council and the Ministers of Education, 2 May 1989 presented by the Commission. European Commission (Luxembourg Office for Official Publications, 1996). Commission Documents COM(96)494.

The European Schools and the European Baccalaureate (Department of Education and Science, 1985).

Education and State Formation: the Rise of Education Systems in England, France and the USA, Andy Green (Macmillan, 1990).

GENERAL

Copyright & Law for Writers, Helen Shay (How To Books, 1996).

How to Start Word Processing, Ian Phillipson (How To Books, 1995).

How to Use the Internet, Graham Jones (How To Books, 1996).

Improving Your Written English, Marion Field (How To Books, 1997).

Index